How to Play Winning Bridge

EDGAR KAPLAN
ALFRED SHEINWOLD

HOW TO PLAY WINNING BRIDGE

New Revised Edition

COLLIER BOOKS
NEW YORK, N.Y.

This Collier Books edition is published
by arrangement with Fleet Publishing Corporation

Collier Books is a division of The Crowell-
Collier Publishing Company

First Collier Books Edition 1962

Library of Congress Catalog Card Number: A62-8702

Hecho en los E.E.U.U.
Printed in the United States of America

Introduction

IT IS appropriate that bridge players should look to the leading players for their advice, and this book is a happy opportunity to do so because its authors finished one-two in the annual race for the master-point championship of the United States.

But I think this book offers an even greater opportunity to bridge students. Bidding methods have been in a state of flux for several years, and authorities have come to be divided into two groups, the conservatives who adhere to the methods of the Thirties and the radicals who insist that every bid must be a post-World War II development. Messrs. Sheinwold and Kaplan have found a happy compromise—the best of the new and the best of the old. And since they have blended it skillfully, it is a very palatable concoction.

To the job of writing this book both of its authors brought all the most desirable ingredients. To teach bridge, one should be a good player, a good writer, and a good teacher. These don't always go together—in fact, they very seldom do. But the Sheinwold-Kaplan combination combines them. Alfred Sheinwold has long been recognized as a leader among bridge writers, as those who read his newspaper articles and his books already know. Edgar Kaplan is a member of the distinguished faculty of the Card School in New York. And their record as players, mentioned above, speaks for itself.

I trust and hope this book will be a best seller, if only because its authors so richly deserve to have it one. A few years ago an unprejudiced observer named the four most pleasant partners among the leading bridge experts. It will not surprise anyone who knows them to be told that both Alfred Sheinwold and Edgar Kaplan were on the list.

ALBERT H. MOREHEAD
Bridge Editor, The New York Times

Foreword to the Collier Books Edition

THE CONDITIONS that prompted us to write this book four years ago still exist: standard American bidding methods are still inadequate against top-flight competition. The best European teams still push us around, even though our experts are unexcelled at the play of the cards.

Our System, as originally presented, is still sound and eminently playable, but we have added a few "variations" at the end of Chapters 2, 3, 4, 5 and 6. If you follow the System, you may disregard the variations, adopt some of them, or adopt them all. Be sure to have a firm agreement with your partner on which variations you have adopted and which you have rejected.

If you do not want to follow the System, either for lack of a suitable partner or for some other reason, you may still find this book well worth reading. You may like our approach to defensive bidding, our scale of raises, the way we handle shutout bids, or some of our new variations. Many of these can be combined with "standard" bidding methods. At worst, you will benefit by gaining a clear understanding of what your opponents mean when they beat you by playing our System.

E. K.
A. S.

Foreword

IN THE 1930s when contract bridge was in its infancy, some twenty different bidding systems clamored for public favor. Gradually, through trial and error and through spectacular head-on matches like the Lenz-Culbertson-Sims battles, defective bidding methods were weeded out; order began to emerge. By the 1940s, Standard American Bidding had achieved virtually complete acceptance.

Known variously as "one-over-one" or the "Culbertson System" or, more lately, as the "Goren System," Standard Bidding was the fruit of the turbulent Thirties, combining the best features of many of the warring methods. By the 40s, just about every expert and every beginner employed this bidding framework. And rightly so, for Standard American Bidding was magnificently successful on every level, even the very highest. American teams consistently defeated European teams using different methods; our bidding was admired and imitated on five continents; the U. S. was king of the bridge world. For us the system wars were over; we had reached a warm, high, sunny plateau and left the battle far below.

Well, now we're in the 60s and we're still on that same plateau. But the sun has started to set and it's getting a bit chilly up here. In successive years, we have lost world championship matches to the English, to the French and to the Italians, and our prestige has never been lower. (In fact, it has been suggested publicly abroad that the European champion should not meet the U. S. champion for the World title, but that the U. S. should enter its team in the European championship.) Standard American Bidding has lost most of its popularity abroad, and even here at home there is widespread disaffection in the ranks. Many new systems and scores of new conventions and gadgets have found favor. In a typical American tournament today, you would be hard put to find three pairs using identical bidding methods out of the hundreds competing. The long Pax-Romana is ending; the walls are crumbling. The rest of the world has moved ahead.

The British and French and Italians who defeated us bid more accurately than we did. Their systems start with an opening bid that has a much narrower range than ours. In Standard American Bidding, an opening bid of one spade can be anything from a balanced minimum to an unbalanced powerhouse. It could be

A. ♠ K Q 10 9 x x x   ♡ A K x   ◇ K x   ♣ x

or

B. ♠ A K J x x   ♡ A Q x x   ◇ Q x x   ♣ x

or

C. ♠ A J x x   ♡ A Q x x   ◇ Q x x   ♣ x x

As a result, opening bidder has the next-to-impossible task of describing with his rebid which of these widely different hands he holds. But in the British "Acol" system, only "B" and "C" are opened one spade; in the Italian "Roman" system only "A" is opened one spade. Starting with a more meaningful opening bid, these systems achieve much greater clarity and precision in the later rounds of bidding.

The British, French, and Italians who defeated us bid more effectively than we did because they never forgot that they had opponents at the table. Standard American Bidding tends to ignore the enemy. "Bid your own cards and let them worry about theirs" was a reasonable credo twenty years ago, but it won't work today. If you open one club with

♠ K x x   ♡ Q x   ◇ A x x   ♣ K J x x x

and partner responds one diamond holding

♠ x x   ♡ x x   ◇ K Q x x x   ♣ Q x x x

you will reach a fine contract—assuming the opponents stay out of the auction. You will bid and make two clubs. But why should the enemy stay out of the auction when you have made it so easy for them to come in, using up almost none of their bidding room? Almost surely, they are cold for four hearts!

Keeping the opponents out of their best contract is fully as important as getting to your own top spot, and no bidding system that forgets this can compete with a style that does not. If the opponents continually jam up your auctions while you leave theirs strictly alone, you are going to lose.

Well, we like to win. The bidding system we present here is designed for two-way action: to harass the enemy on losing hands; to reach a maximum contract with accuracy and comfort on winning hands. We accomplish this by applying two underlying principles—

1. *Every Sequence of Bids Must Have a Narrowly Defined Meaning.* This is to give us the "accuracy and comfort" on our offensive auctions, enabling us to be sure at all times of just what partner means by every bid. We start with narrowly defined opening bids and extend this greater precision to all our bidding.

2. *Where Safety Permits, High Bids Must Be Used to Describe Weaker Hands, Low Bids to Describe Stronger Hands.* This is to rob the opponents of bidding room on competitive auctions, while leaving ourselves all possible space for delicate investigation when the hand clearly "belongs" to us.

These twin goals—increased accuracy for our strong hands, and greater pre-emption for our weak and average hands—condition our whole bidding style. You will find that many bidding sequences which have wide, nebulous ranges in Standard Bidding show specific values in our framework. And you will find that we get up high very fast with light hands in many situations where Standard Bidding keeps you low. (In the earlier example, we bid not 1 ♣—1 ◇, but 1 NT—3 ◇.) These goals will be restated and applied time and time again in the pages which follow.

It is the application of these two principles to the full range of bidding that is the signal contribution of our system. Very few of the individual bidding devices recommended are original. The weak notrump has been played since the earliest days of the game. Five-card majors, preemptive jumps, weak two-bids, controlled psychics—all have been widely used by many others. We are advocates not of the separate ingredients, but of the whole concoction.

Superficially, our bidding system resembles that of Alvin Roth and Tobias Stone, the pioneers of modern American bidding. However, this resemblance is more apparent than real—many of the devices are the same, but the underlying structure is quite different. The very core of the Roth-Stone System is the Sound Opening Bid. Roth-Stone players pass many hands which are opened in other systems, and thereby achieve great accuracy in bidding the hands they do open. In contrast, our system is controlled not by the sound opening but by the weak notrump and by the five-card major. We enjoy the increased precision that comes from limiting the opening bid, but do not sacrifice the advantage of initiative that comes from getting in the first blow with minimum 'hands. We feel that we have the best of both worlds.

Still, it would be unthinkable not to acknowledge our great debt to Roth and Stone who, in blazing the trail away from Standard Bidding, made such valuable contributions. They were among the first to realize that many jump bids should be used to describe weak hands. And theirs, too, is the conception of the forcing 1 NT response to the five-card major opening, which has become the cornerstone of our major-suit bidding.

We are grateful also to the select group of leading Eastern experts who helped us test our theories in the fire of competition. Ivar Stakgold and Sol Rubinow with their young Boston group, Norman Kay in Philadelphia, and, in New York, Leonard Harmon, Dick Kahn and that enthusiastic weak notrump addict, Ralph Hirschberg—all have helped formulate and perfect our System.

E. K.

A. S.

Contents

How to Play Winning Bridge

Chapter 1

The Opening Bid

GENERAL

EVERY BIDDING SYSTEM in bridge is built around the opening bid. Alter your conception of the opening bid in any particular, however slight, and you will see something very strange happen. Responder's bids will take on slightly different shades of meaning to keep step with the opening. Opener's rebids will be affected both by the new opening bids and by the new responses. Soon this ripple of change will spread through your entire bidding structure, and you will find yourself playing a new system.

This is the experience we had when we started to play the 12- to 14-point opening notrump, the "weak notrump." It didn't seem like such a drastic change at first—we gave up the 16- to 18-point "strong notrump" and with an occasional balanced minimum, if it looked like just the right hand, we would use our new gadget.

The results were excellent when we opened with the weak notrump, but we found that many auctions that did not start with the weak notrump were being affected.

How should we describe the 16- to 18-point hand, now that it couldn't be opened 1 NT? We decided that opener would show a balanced hand too strong for a 12- to 14-point 1 NT opening when he first bid a suit and later bid notrump.

Then what was opener to rebid with balanced 12- to 14-point hands that he had chosen to open in a suit? The only answer we could accept was startling: *All our balanced minimums had to be opened with the weak notrump,* for the weak rebid of 1 NT was denied us. Now, close to one in every four hands we opened was opened 1 NT.

Next, we discovered that we were no longer opening in four-card major suits. Why not? Well, there are only two good reasons for opening one heart or one spade without a five-card suit:

1. *To Prepare a Rebid*. In standard bidding, you dare not open

♠ AQxx   ♡ Qxx   ◊ A10xx   ♣ xx

with one diamond for you have no reasonable rebid over a two-club response; you are too weak to rebid either two notrump or two spades. Therefore, you solve your problem in advance and open one spade. But we open this hand 1 NT, not one spade or one diamond. And if our hand has the same pattern but is too strong for a weak notrump opening

♠ AQxx   ♡ Qxx   ◊ A10xx   ♣ Kx

then we are strong enough to open one diamond and rebid 2 NT over two clubs. It is the hands that we open with 1 NT that present rebidding problems in standard bidding. Stronger hands take care of themselves.

2. *For Pre-emptive Effect*. Ordinarily, you might well open a light hand like

♠ KQxx   ♡ Jx   ◊ xxx   ♣ AQxx

with one spade, especially in third or fourth seat, in order to try to shut the opponents out. But we open this hand 1 NT and really make it tough for the enemy to come in. And if we are too strong for a weak notrump

♠ KQxx   ♡ Jx   ◊ Axx   ♣ AQxx

we open one club, welcome the opponents into the auction, and bare our fangs.

Since we had no use for the opening in a four-card major, we would have been foolish to deny ourselves the ease and comfort of playing "five-card majors," guaranteeing at least a five-card suit with the opening bid of one heart or one spade.

All this affected our minor-suit opening bids too. No longer would one-club or one-diamond openings be made with flat, minimum hands—these were opened 1 NT. The minor-suit opening was either a strong balanced hand or else had some distributional feature—a singleton, a good side suit—to make it unsuitable for a notrump opening. Thus the minimum strength for a one-club or a one-diamond bid became greater than for either a weak-notrump or a major-suit opening.

The end product of this process was a System in which bidding could be more accurate because it started with an opening bid that gave more information. Actually, it might be considered that what we present here is *three* systems—three separate, self-contained bidding methods, each one initiated by one of our three distinct opening one-bids: the weak notrump, the major-suit opening, the minor-suit opening. Each type of opening bid has its own requirements in distributional pattern, overall strength and high-card structure.

Overall strength we will talk of in terms of points, figured on the standard Work point-count: ace—4; king—3; queen —2; jack—1. However, points are only the flesh and sinew of a hand. For an opening bid, we always look beneath the flesh to the skeleton—the high-card structure. This we value on a simple Quick Trick table: ace-king—2; ace-queen—1½; ace—1; king-queen—1; king—½.

Opening bid requirements will be expressed throughout in terms of points, but we correct for Quick Tricks. With 3 QT or more, a hand qualifies for an opening regardless of how much flesh is on the bones. With 2½ QT, you may open one point light. With 2 QT, normal rules apply. With 1½ QT an opening is only optional at best and requires an extra point. With 1 QT or less, don't open the bidding.

These corrections apply to the minimum requirements for all three types of opening bid.

♠ A Q J x   ♡ Q J x x   ♢ Q x x   ♣ J x
   —13 points, 1½ QT.

♠ A K x x   ♡ K x x x   ♢ K x x   ♣ x x
   —13 points, 3 QT.

♠ A Q x x x   ♡ A Q x x   ♢ x x   ♣ x x
   —12 points, 3 QT.

♠ A x x x x   ♡ A x x x   ♢ Q x   ♣ Q x
   —12 points, 2 QT.

THE WEAK NOTRUMP

The first requirement for an opening of 1 NT is balanced distribution. "Balanced" and "unbalanced" are terms we will be using throughout this work, so let's be specific. By "balanced" we mean a hand that has relatively even distribution—4-3-3-3 or 4-4-3-2. No five-card suit or single-ton. By "unbalanced" we mean a hand that has a void, a singleton or a six-card or longer suit. You will notice that the 5-3-3-2 and 5-4-2-2 distributions fall into neither group. These we call "semibalanced" and may on occasion treat them as either balanced or unbalanced hands.

These are balanced:

♠ A x x   ♡ K x x x   ◇ Q J x   ♣ x x x
♠ x x   ♡ A K x x   ◇ A Q x x   ♣ x x x

These are semibalanced:

♠ x x   ♡ Q x   ◇ A J x x   ♣ A 10 x x x
♠ A Q 10 x x   ♡ K x   ◇ J x x   ♣ x x x

These are unbalanced:

♠ A K J x x x   ♡ Q x x   ◇ x x   ♣ x x
♠ x   ♡ K x x x   ◇ K J x x   ♣ K x x x

The point-count range for the weak notrump is 12 to 14 points. Any balanced hand within these limits must be opened 1 NT, if it is to be opened at all. You may, if you wish, pass a hand which qualifies for a weak notrump (if you are vulnerable and the opponents are not, it is often wise to pass 12-point hands that are not rich in tens and nines). But you may never open with a suit bid on a bal-anced 12- to 14-point hand. As you will see later, the Sys-tem will bite you if you do.

Note that it is your distributional pattern that is of par-amount importance, not the location of your high cards. There is no requirement of stoppers in all suits or even three suits. Nor is a weak doubleton in any suit a deterrent to the weak notrump opening. If your distribution is 4-3-3-3 or 4-4-3-2 and your count is 12 to 14 points, you open 1 NT.

However, remember the Quick Trick correction. With 2½ QT you may open with 11 points. With 1½ QT you need 13 points to open. With 1 QT or less, don't bother to count your points; you don't have an opening bid.

♠ K x x   ♡ Q 10 x x   ◇ A x x   ♣ K J x

A perfect "book" weak notrump opening. 13 points and 2 QT.

♠ K Q x x   ♡ K x x x   ◇ J x x   ♣ A x

Two four-card majors are no bar. With a balanced hand and 13 points (and 2½ QT) you must open 1 NT.

♠ xx ♡ AQx ◇ Kxxx ♣ QJxx

Don't worry about the spade holding. Open 1 NT. This hand, however, you might elect to pass if vulnerable.

♠ QJx ♡ KJxx ◇ KJx ♣ Qxx

You have 13 points and should pass all 13 of 'em. You have only 1 QT and so cannot open.

♠ A10xx ♡ Kxx ◇ Axx ♣ xxx

Open 1 NT. You have only 11 points, but with 2½ QT you may open one point lighter.

With the semibalanced 5-3-3-2 and 5-4-2-2 distributions, and 12 to 14 points, you must decide whether or not to open 1 NT. If the five-card suit is spades or hearts you should almost never open 1 NT; preference is given to the major-suit opening.

With 5-3-3-2 distribution and a five-card minor suit, your tendency should be to treat the hand as balanced and open 1 NT. Only if the hand contains a top-heavy suit and is close to 14 points should you treat it as unbalanced and open one club or one diamond.

5-4-2-2 distributions, however, should more often be treated as *un*balanced. Only if the point count is concentrated in the doubletons and if the long suits are weak should a 1 NT opening be considered. When both long suits are minors, the 1 NT opening may be regarded with a somewhat less jaundiced eye, but even here a suit opening is usually better.

♠ AQxxx ♡ Kxx ◇ xxx ♣ Kx

Do not open 1 NT. You have a fine major suit, and as you will see, may open one spade.

♠ Kxx ♡ xxx ◇ AQxxx ♣ Kx

Treat this as balanced and open 1 NT. With 5-3-3-2 distribution, 1 NT is preferred to a minor-suit opening when the hand is weak and spread thin.

♠ xx ♡ AJx ◇ AKQxx ♣ xxx

Treat this hand as unbalanced and open one diamond, not 1 NT. The hand is strong and concentrated.

♠ Q 10 x x   ♡ x x   ◇ A Q J x x   ♣ A x

Do not open 1 NT. With 5-4-2-2 distribution you should generally bid a suit. Open one diamond.

♠ K x   ♡ A Q   ◇ Q 10 x x   ♣ J x x x x

This is the exceptional 5-4-2-2 hand that is opened 1 NT. You have 9 points in your doubletons and weak long suits.

THE MAJOR-SUIT OPENING

The opening bid of one spade or one heart promises five (or more) cards in the suit opened. This requirement is basic and invariable—if you do not have a five-card major, you may open 1 NT, 1 ♣ or 1 ◇, but never 1 ♡ or 1 ♠.

However, once the suit requirements are met, just about any hand that looks good to you probably qualifies for a major-suit opening bid. In deciding whether to open the bidding, you must consider the same three factors: Your point count, your Quick Tricks, your distribution.

A point count of 12 gives you a minimum opening bid in a major, just as it gives you a weak notrump opening. However, for a one-heart or one-spade opening, you may have as little as 9 or 10 (even, conceivably, 8) high-card points. The difference can be made up in the points you add for distributional features. These features may be long suits and/or short suits; any unbalanced hand gets extra points.

ADD 1 POINT: for a 6-card suit; for a singleton.
ADD 2 POINTS: for a 7-card suit; for a void.

Add these distribution points to your high-card points, and if the total reaches 12 you probably have an opening bid.

Why only "probably"? Because, although points are nice to hold, no point ever took a trick. Aces and kings do take tricks—lots of them—and take them on defense as well as offense. So let's go back to the Quick Trick table: ace-king —2; ace-queen—1½; ace—1; king-queen—1; K x—½, and remember that (1) a hand with 2½ Quick Tricks or more is opened with 11 points and (2) no hand with less than 2 Quick Tricks is much of an opening bid, but a hand with 1½ QT may be opened if you have 13 points.

Here are a few rock-bottom minimum major-suit opening bids. Unless you're a very unlucky card-holder, you'll generally have a little extra.

♠ K Q 10 x x   ♥ K Q x   ♦ Q x x   ♣ x x

Open one spade. This "semibalanced" hand gets no credit for distribution, but it has 12 high-card points and 2 QT.

♠ A K J x x   ♥ x   ♦ x x x   ♣ Q J x x

Open one spade. You have 11 points in high cards plus 1 point for the singleton, making 12.

♠ A K x x x x x   ♥ Q 10 x   ♦ x x   ♣ x

Open one spade. Add to your 9 high-card points 2 points for your seven-card suit and 1 point for your singleton. You have 12 in all.

♠ A Q 10 x x   ♥ A J x x   ♦ x x   ♣ x x

Open one spade. You have no extra points for distribution, but your 11 points in high cards are sufficient with 2½ QT.

♠ K J 10 x x x   ♥ A J 10 x   ♦ J x x   ♣ none

Open one spade. This is optional. You have only 1½ QT, but 13 points—10 in high cards, 2 for the void, 1 for the six-card suit. The ♠ 10 and ♥ 10 would induce us to open.

♠ Q J x x x   ♥ K x x   ♦ K Q x   ♣ J x

Pass. You have 12 points in high cards, but nothing for distribution and only 1½ QT.

♠ x x x x x   ♥ K x x   ♦ K Q x   ♣ A x

Open 1 NT. This is that rarity—a weak notrump with a five-card major. These conditions must be present: a worthless suit, 5-3-3-2 distribution, honors in the other three suits.

THE MINOR-SUIT OPENING

An opening bid of one club or one diamond may be made with any type of distribution—balanced, semibalanced or unbalanced. With a balanced hand, a minor suit opening is made when the hand is too strong for a weak notrump —15 points or more in high cards. With an unbalanced hand, a minor suit is opened when no long major suit is held.

In either case, balanced or unbalanced, the one-club or one-diamond opening bid describes a good hand, for we do not open the scrawny minimum hands in the minors that we do in the majors. Why not? A light opening in a major may get you to a "thin" but makeable 10-trick game, but to take the 11 tricks for a minor-suit game you must have solid values. What's more, a skinny opening of one heart or one spade may make it difficult for the enemy to contest the auction, whereas a one-club or one-diamond opening has little pre-emptive value. You can't fight tanks with pillows.

Converted into figures, this means that you need at least 14 points, not 12 points, to open with an unbalanced minor-suit hand. Compute your points just as for a major-suit opening—add to your high-card points 2 points for a seven-card suit and for a void, 1 point for a six-card suit and for a singleton. Correct for high-card structure—with 3 QT open regardless of points; with 2½ QT, open with 13 points; with less than 2 QT don't open.

There is one special rule for unbalanced minor suit openings: add one point for the possession of a four-card spade suit. This is because a secondary spade suit makes any hand easy to rebid and of greater competitive value.

These are rock-bottom minimum minor-suit openings:

♠ x   ♡ KQxx   ♢ KQ10xx   ♣ QJx

Open one diamond. This hand just qualifies, with 13 points in high cards plus one point for the singleton.

♠ AJxx   ♡ xx   ♢ xx   ♣ AQJxx

Open one club. You have 13 points—12 in high cards and one for the four-card spade suit. With 2½ QT, 13 points suffices.

♠ Qxx   ♡ Qxxx   ♢ AK10xxx   ♣ none

Open one diamond. 11 points in high cards plus 2 points for the void plus 1 point for the six-card suit equal 14 points and an opening bid.

♠ xxx   ♡ x   ◇ Axxx   ♣ AKxxx

Open one club. With 3 QT it is mandatory to open.

These next hands, however, do not meet the specifications:

♠ KJxx   ♡ xx   ◇ x   ♣ AQ10xxx

Pass this strong playing hand, intending to overcall later. You have only 13 points—10 in high cards and 1 each for the singleton, the six-card suit, the four-card spade suit.

♠ KQx   ♡ x   ◇ Qx   ♣ KJ10xxxx

Pass. You have 11 points in high cards and 3 in distribution, but with only 1½ QT you may not open in a minor.

♠ xxx   ♡ xxx   ◇ AKJxx   ♣ Ax

Open one notrump, not one diamond. With 3 QT you must open, but you should prefer the limited one notrump opening (with a semibalanced hand) to a substandard minor-suit bid.

If you have the requirements for a minor-suit opening, which suit do you bid? Rarely will you have a difficult choice between opening one club and one diamond when you have an unbalanced hand—you simply open your five-card suit. When you hold both a long diamond suit and a long club suit, you open one diamond. Later, when you bid your club suit, partner can take you back to diamonds without increasing the level. These hands present no problem. However, a special situation is created by one type of distribution: Three four-card suits and a singleton.

The 4-4-4-1 distribution is unique—it is unbalanced because of the singleton, but contains no long suit. This means that you cannot open one notrump, being unbalanced; you cannot open one spade or one heart, having no five-card major; you must open one club or one diamond with a four-card suit. Which do you open?

Clearly, with two four-card majors (♠ AQxx ♡ Axxx ◇ QJxx ♣ x) you have only one four-card minor, and you bid it. With one major and both minors

(♠ A Q x x ♡ x ◇ A x x x ♣ Q J x x) it is generally
better to open one club than to open one diamond, for the
lower bid gives the partnership its maximum chance to find
a fit.

Many authorities will tell you to open one diamond, the
suit under the singleton, with this pattern. Their theory is
that this makes it easy for you to bid all three of your suits:
you open one diamond; partner responds one heart. You
rebid one spade, and bid your clubs over partner's next bid.

The fallacy here is that the hand is not strong enough
for three bids. If, over your one-spade rebid, partner bids
1 NT, two diamonds, two hearts or two spades, you will
pass and leave clubs unbid. So you might as well open one
club in the first place and give partner all possible room
for his initial response. As a general rule, *open 4-4-4-1
hands in your lowest ranking suit.*

The requirements for opening with the 4-4-4-1 pattern
are the same as for all unbalanced minor-suit hands. With
a singleton spade, you need 13 points in high cards to add
to your 1 point for unbalance. With any other singleton,
you need only 12 points in high cards, for you get one
extra point for your four-card spade suit. As always, with
2½ QT these requirements are lowered by one point.

♠ K Q 10 x   ♡ Q J x x   ◇ A x x x   ♣ x

Open one diamond. You have 12 points in high cards,
one point for the singleton, one point for the four-card
spade suit. You may not open one spade or one heart with
only four-card suits, and your singleton bars a 1 NT opening.

♠ x   ♡ K Q 10 x   ◇ Q J x x   ♣ A x x x

Pass. Without the spade suit, you have only 13 points.
If the opponents bid spades, you can back into the auction,
after passing, with a takeout double.

♠ Q J x x   ♡ x   ◇ A Q 10 x   ♣ K Q x x

Open one club. With 4-4-4-1, open in your lowest ranking suit.

STRONG BALANCED HANDS

There is another whole family of hands which you open
with one club or one diamond. These are the balanced
hands too strong for the weak notrump opening. The weak

notrump takes care of your balanced hands of 14 points or less; with all other balanced hands, from 15 to 20 points, you open in a minor suit.

♠ A Q 10 x   ♡ K x   ◇ Q x x   ♣ A J x x

Open one club. Your spade suit is too short for a one-spade opening; your 16-point hand too strong for a 1 NT opening.

With balanced strong hands, just as with 4-4-4-1 hands, you may have the problem of whether to open one club or one diamond. Not, of course, with the example just cited, but change it to

♠ K x   ♡ Q x x   ◇ A J x x   ♣ A Q 10 x

and what would you bid?

Here again, you open one club, not one diamond, and for much the same reason as before. The only reason for bidding the higher ranking of touching suits first is to make it convenient to get a preference from partner when you bid your second suit next. But no matter whether you open one club or one diamond, *you don't intend to bid your second suit next;* you intend to rebid 1 NT over a one-heart or one-spade response. So there is no reason to bid diamonds first.

By opening one club you give yourself two chances to find a suit fit quickly: responder can raise clubs or bid one diamond. However, by opening one diamond you would make it difficult for responder to bid clubs, so you would cut in half your chance of finding a quick fit.

Quite often you will hold a strong balanced hand without a four-card holding in either minor suit. You might have two four-card majors, or a hand distributed 4-3-3-3 with one four-card major.

What do you open with these hands?

1. ♠ A K x x   ♡ K Q x x   ◇ x x   ♣ K Q x

2. ♠ A K x x   ♡ K Q x   ◇ x x x   ♣ K Q x

You must open in a *three*-card minor; you should bid one club.

There is nothing novel or daring about a three-card minor opening. In fact, if you take the ace of spades out of each of the previous examples—

1. ♠ K x x x   ♡ K Q x x   ◇ x x   ♣ K Q x

2. ♠ K x x x   ♡ K Q x   ◇ x x x   ♣ K Q x

"standard bidding" would open both hands with one club. (We, of course, would now open 1 NT.) It is true that, since we play five-card majors, we open in three-card minors a little more frequently than is the standard practice. But we have a built-in safety factor. *Whenever we open in a three-card minor, we have a strong hand—too good for 1 NT.* "Standard bidding" opens in three-card minors on *weak* hands—not good enough for a strong notrump bid.

Very, very seldom will opening in a three-card minor lead to trouble, but it does happen. If you are in trouble, it can't be very serious when your opening one club bid is

♠ A K x x   ♡ K Q x   ◇ x x x   ♣ K Q x

It can be a disaster when your opening one-club bid is

♠ K x x x   ♡ K Q x   ◇ x x x   ♣ K Q x.

And your extra strength is not your only protection. As you will see in the chapter on "After a Minor-Suit Opening," responder will always allow for the possibility of a three-card minor opening. There are adequate safeguards.

With two three-card minors to choose between, you should almost always open one club. Only with very good diamonds and worthless clubs should you prefer to open one diamond. The normal occasion for opening a three-card diamond suit is when you hold two four-card majors, three diamonds and two clubs:

♠ A Q x x   ♡ K J x x   ◇ K x x   ♣ A x

Never open in a *two*-card suit—it is impossible for responder to catch such a curve ball. Remember, the minor suit opening is not artificial. Under certain carefully controlled conditions, you may find yourself playing a high contract in the suit you open.

Here are a few examples of three-card minor suit openings:

♠ Q 10 x x   ♡ A Q x   ◇ A Q x   ♣ K x x

Open one club. Even though your diamonds are a little stronger than your clubs, open in the lower ranking suit.

♠ KQ10x   ♡ AQx   ◇ AQx   ♣ xxx

Open one diamond. This is the exceptional hand with which you prefer diamonds to clubs with three in each suit. Whenever possible, avoid opening in a three-card suit without a high honor, as it makes it impossible to determine whether or not you have the suit stopped for a notrump contract.

♠ AJxx   ♡ KJxx   ◇ Jxx   ♣ AQ

Open one diamond. Your clubs are very much stronger than your diamonds, but you may not bid a two-card suit. Nor may you bid a four-card major or a 16-point notrump, so you have no option.

WHY?

This concludes our treatment of opening one-bids—the minimum requirements for opening each type of bid, and which suit to open with. But before we leave the one-bids, something more should be said about the "why" of all this. What do we gain by such a major alteration in opening bid style?

Primarily, we gain accuracy in bidding games and slams. This increased accuracy stems directly from the fact that the opening bid carries with it so much more information. Take, for example, the opening one-spade bid in "standard bidding." It can be made with either of two quite dissimilar types of hand.

TYPE 1: ♠ AK10x   ♡ Qxx   ◇ Kxxx   ♣ xx

TYPE 2: ♠ KQJxx   ♡ AJx   ◇ x   ♣ Qxxx

We, however, open Type 1 hands with 1 NT, thereby eliminating some 40 per cent of all "standard bidding" one-spade openings. With such a tremendous head-start, we can be a great deal more precise in our handling of the other 60 per cent, the Type 2 hands, which we do open with one spade.

Now examine these two "standard bidding" auctions.

I. ♠ A x x   ♠ J x x x
   ♥ x x   ♥ Q J x
   ♦ K Q x x x   ♦ x x
   ♣ K x x   ♣ A Q x x

OPENER	RESPONDER
1 ♦	1 ♠
2 ♠	?

What should responder do over two spades? Well, if you go by the result, he had better pass, as he is probably too high already. But what if opener, for the identical sequence, held:

II. ♠ K Q x x   ♠ J x x x
   ♥ K x   ♥ Q J x
   ♦ A Q x x x   ♦ x x
   ♣ x x   ♣ A Q x x

OPENER	RESPONDER
1 ♦	1 ♠
2 ♠	?

With a little luck, eleven tricks can be made. Clearly, if *this* is opener's hand, responder must bid over two spades. How can responder make an intelligent decision when his partner, in "standard bidding" might have *either* hand? The fault lies in the too-broad range of the opening one-diamond bid. Opener simply does not have enough rebids available to tell partner which of the many different "standard bidding" one-diamond openings he holds.

We, however, don't have this problem, for the range of our one-diamond opening is narrower. With opener's hand in "Hand I" we would have opened with 1 NT, not one diamond, and that would have been the end of the auction. With "Hand II" our bidding would start as shown, and responder would proceed confidently to game. He would not be *gambling* on finding opener with a good hand. He would *know* how strong a hand opener held.

You will see in the next few chapters just how we manage to convert the narrower meaning we have given to the opening bids of one in a suit into more accurate bidding sequences—more games and slams bid and made. This is the greatest gift of the weak 1 NT opening—you will have fine results when you use it, *but its most striking benefits come when you open in a suit.* For it is the weak notrump which makes our whole system possible, cutting down the broad ranges of the suit opening bids by eliminating all balanced minimum hands.

The weak notrump itself, in contrast to most of our bids, does not always aim at precision. Of course, in game-going and slam auctions, you can bid as delicately as you want to. However, when responder is too weak to look for game, you sacrifice almost all chance to investigate the best fit for a suit contract when you open 1 NT. For example, in "standard bidding" a partnership could reach a contract of two hearts with these cards:

♠ A x	♠ x x x
♡ K Q x x	♡ A J x x
◇ J x x	◇ x x
♣ K x x x	♣ Q J x x

OPENER	RESPONDER
1 ♣	1 ♡
2 ♡	Pass

Two hearts is a fine contract; with normal splits you will make an overtrick. We, however, would bid one notrump with opener's hand and be passed out there. With a spade or diamond opening lead, we could be set two tricks. Now on the surface this looks like a major defeat for the weak notrump—one notrump down two instead of two hearts making three! But look at the complete hand, which is taken from a team-of-four match we played in the National Championships last year.

West dealer.
North-South vulnerable.

```
              NORTH
            ♠ K x x x
            ♡ 1 0 9 8 x
            ◇ A K 10
            ♣ x x
```

	WEST		EAST
	♠ A x		♠ x x x
	♡ K Q x x		♡ A J x x
	◇ J x x		◇ x x
	♣ K x x x		♣ Q J x x

	SOUTH
	♠ Q J 10 x
	♡ x
	◇ Q x x x x
	♣ A x x

WEST	NORTH	EAST	SOUTH
1 ♣	Double	Pass	2 ♣
Pass	2 ♠	3 ♣	4 ♠
Pass	Pass	Pass	

The auction is given as it occurred with our teammates sitting North and South and our opponents East and West. Our teammates made their vulnerable game contract with ease, losing one trick each in spades, hearts, and clubs. However, when the hand was replayed at our table, this was the auction (we sat East and West, our opponents North and South):

WEST	NORTH	EAST	SOUTH
1 NT	Pass	Pass	Pass

Neither of our vulnerable opponents could risk a bid at the two-level. We would cheerfully have given them the 100 points for setting us two tricks when they could have scored a vulnerable game worth 620 points. But they didn't even get that. Who can blame North for leading the ♡ 10 against 1 NT? He had a blind lead to make, with no auction to guide him, and guessed wrong. So we made our 1 NT contract. South shifted to diamonds on winning the ♣ A, but our opponents could now take only six tricks before we took seven!

This hand points up two features which work in favor of the weak notrump. The first is *pre-emption*. When you have a minimum balanced opening, you should want to make it as difficult as possible for the opponents to enter the auction. It is all very well to explore carefully to find a suit fit with partner, but you will discover, in general, that *if you and your partner have good fitting hands, so have your opponents.* With a light opening bid, your first concern must be buying the contract cheap, not reaching your maximum spot. Only with a strong hand can you afford to probe delicately for a fit, safe in the knowledge that you can outbid the enemy. And yet this strong 16- to 18-point hand is opened 1 NT in "standard bidding," making it difficult to find your fit, while the weak 12-14 point hand is opened one club, making it easy for the opponents to compete.

The second feature of the weak notrump which shows up in our example hand is the trouble it gives the opponents on defense. When no suits have been bid, declarer has a tremendous advantage over the defenders. He *knows* which suits to attack and which to avoid; they must guess. Even against the most expert opponents it is worth, on average, between one and two tricks in the play to reach your final contract without bidding any suits (1 NT—3 NT, 1 NT—Pass).

Naturally, this is just as true of the strong 16-18-point notrump opening. But you hold far fewer 17-point hands than 13-point hands. And it is with the weaker hands that you are more likely to need a little friendly defense.

This, then is the gist of our system: We give up accuracy in our partial bidding when we have balanced minimum openings; in return, we gain accuracy for slam, game, and partial bidding when we have strong and unbalanced openings. In addition, we gain pre-emption for our bad hands.

You will find this theme repeated many times and in many ways throughout our bidding system—HIGH, PRE-EMPTIVE BIDDING FOR WEAKER HANDS: "KEEP-IT-LOW," PRECISE BIDDING FOR STRONGER HANDS.

Chapter 2

Other Opening Bids

NOT ALL TYPES of opening bid were covered in the first chapter. Let us tie up all the loose ends here with a discussion of Very Strong Openings, Pre-emptive Openings, Openings After Partner Has Passed, and Psychic Openings.

THE FORCING 2 ♣

Once in a while, if you're lucky, you'll hold a hand so strong that you're afraid to open at the one-level—partner might pass when you can make game. Here you can employ the artificial bid of 2 ♣, our only forcing opening.

This bid has nothing whatever to do with clubs. It merely announces some sort of very strong hand and forces responder to keep the auction alive so that opener will get a chance to tell his story. Opener can have any distribution from 4-3-3-3 to 7-6-0-0. His subsequent bidding will clarify his holding.

    ♠ A K x   ♡ A Q J x   ◇ A K Q x   ♣ K x

Open 2 ♣. You want to play no lower than 3 NT no matter what sort of Yarborough partner holds, so you can't risk a 1 ◇ opening, which might be passed.

    ♠ A K Q 10 x x   ♡ A K Q x x   ◇ x   ♣ x

Open 2 ♣. With this enormous playing strength you must make sure that you reach game at least.

The response of 2 ◇ to an opening bid of 2 ♣ is an artificial bid of denial. It says nothing at all about responder's diamond holding; its message is the wet blanket. "Partner," it says, "I'm certainly glad to hear that you're so strong, but be careful. I have a horrid hand."

Any other response to a 2 ♣ opening bid shows strength. Bids of 2 ♡, 2 ♠, 3 ♣ and 3 ◇ are constructive, natural responses, promising length in the bid suit and 8 points or more in high cards. (With a really long suit headed by two high honors, the point-count can be shaded down.) The response of 2 NT is a limited bid showing 7 to 10 points, a balanced hand and no strong suit. Here are a few examples of responses to a 2 ♣ opening:

    ♠ Kxxx   ♡ xxx   ◇ xxx   ♣ Jxx

Respond 2 ◇.

    ♠ KJxxx   ♡ xxx   ◇ xx   ♣ Jxx

Respond 2 ◇.

    ♠ KJxxx   ♡ Axx   ◇ xx   ♣ Jxx

Respond 2 ♠.

    ♠ KQJxxx   ♡ xx   ◇ xxx   ♣ xx

Respond 2 ♠.

    ♠ Kxxx   ♡ Kxx   ◇ Qxx   ♣ Jxx

Respond 2 NT.

A positive response to the 2 ♣ opening means that a slam is in view, so these auctions are treated further under "Slam Bidding." Right here, let's see how opener describes his hand after the negative 2 ◇ response.

A. *Unbalanced Strong Hands*

If opener has a long suit—

    ♠ AKQxxx   ♡ AKx   ◇ Axx   ♣ x

he bids it over 2 ◇.

OPENER	RESPONDER
2 ♣	2 ◇
2 ♠	

Holding a two-suiter—

    ♠ AKQxxx   ♡ AKxxx   ◇ A   ♣ x

he starts to bid his suits in ranking order.

OPENER	RESPONDER
2 ♣	2 ◊
2 ♠	2 NT
3 ♡	

Note that it is not necessary for opening bidder to jump. Every time he bids a new suit, he forces responder to keep the bidding open, for opener's hand is unlimited. However, the 2 ♣ bidder can give responder a chance to pass under game with a worthless hand. This he does by rebidding his suit at the first opportunity, thereby limiting his hand.

♠ A K Q x x x	♠ x
♡ A K x	♡ 10 x x x
◊ A x x	◊ J x x x
♣ x	♣ x x x x

OPENER	RESPONDER
2 ♣	2 ◊
2 ♠	2 NT
3 ♠	Pass

Opener is too powerful to bid merely 1 ♠ so he uses the forcing 2 ♣. Responder, naturally, bids the negative 2 ◊. Opener now shows his suit, and responder, forced to reply, signs off again with 2 NT. Opener cannot make game facing a valueless hand, so he rebids his suit to give responder a chance to pass, an opportunity gratefully accepted.

But were opener's hand

♠ A K Q x x x x   ♡ A K x   ◊ A x   ♣ x

he would jump to 4 ♠ over 2 NT, for now he *can* make game opposite a bust.

B. *Balanced Strong Hands*

When opener has a balanced or semibalanced powerhouse of 25 or 26 points

♠ K Q   ♡ A Q J x   ◊ K Q J x   ♣ A K x

he bids 3 NT over 2 ◊.

OPENER	RESPONDER
2 ♣	2 ◊
3 NT	

With a little less, opener will give his partner a chance to quit under game. This he does by bidding 2 NT, not 3 NT, over the 2 ◊ response. Now he describes a balanced or semibalanced hand of 23 or 24 points. Three or four points in responder's hand will suffice for game.

♠ KQ	♠ Jxx
♡ AQJx	♡ xx
◊ KJxx	◊ Qxxx
♣ AKx	♣ xxxx

OPENER	RESPONDER
2 ♣	2 ◊
2 NT	3 NT
Pass	

Having 23 points, opener first bids 2 ♣, then rebids 2 NT. Responder signs off with 2 ◊ at his first turn, but carries on to game over 2 NT, as he is not completely valueless. Without the queen, responder would pass over 2 NT.

There is also available a slightly weaker opening bid for a strong balanced hand. Instead of opening 2 ♣ and rebidding 2 NT, opener can start with the *opening* bid of 2 NT. This describes a balanced or semibalanced hand of 21 or 22 points. A five-card suit, even in a major, is no deterrent to a 2 NT opening if the point-count is right. In fact, you may open 2 NT with as little as 20 points in high cards if your hand contains a strong five-card suit. Responder, to raise the 2 NT opening to 3 NT, needs 5 points or more.

♠ AJxxx	♠ xx
♡ AKx	♡ Jxxx
◊ QJx	◊ xxxx
♣ AQ	♣ Kxx

OPENER	RESPONDER
2 NT	Pass

Opener, with 21 points in a semibalanced hand, bids 2 NT. Responder, with 4 points and no good suit, is too weak to go to game.

You will notice that opener has a continuous range of bids for strong balanced and semibalanced hands:

> 21 or 22 points—open 2 NT
> 23 or 24 points—open 2 ♣; rebid 2 NT
> 25 or 26 points—open 2 ♣; rebid 3 NT

And if some day you hold 27 or 28 points in a balanced hand, you can describe it with the opening bid of 3 NT. We use this clumsy bid for a hand which virtually never appears because a 3 NT opening makes slam investigation very difficult.

PRE-EMPTIVE OPENING BIDS

At the other end of the spectrum are the weak pre-emptive opening bids: all suit openings higher than the one-level from 2 ◇ up to 5 ◇. There is a lot of variety in this range—the "weak 2-bids": 2 ◇, 2 ♡, 2 ♠; the opening 3-bids: 3 ♣, 3 ◇, 3 ♡, 3 ♠; 4-bids in minors: 4 ♣, 4 ◇; opening game bids: 4 ♡, 4 ♠, 5 ♣, 5 ◇ —and each class of pre-empt is distinct from the others. But all have in common an element of *fear*—fear that the opponents can make a game or slam, if allowed the bidding room to get together.

The underlying theory of pre-emptive bidding is that when your hand will take tricks only with your long suit as trump, it is safe for you to make a very high bid on a weak hand. Of course, you can be doubled and set 500 or 700 or 900 points if partner is weak also. But if partner does not have the strength to avert a big set, the opponents could surely make game or slam. And this is your safety, for it is no loss to be set 500 points if the opponents have a game, or even 900 points if they have a slam.

True, it is no gain either. But your profit comes when the opponents, put under pressure by your pre-emptive bid and forced to make a critical decision in the blind at a high level, go wrong. They may double you when they should bid for their own contract; they may be crowded out of bidding a good slam or pushed into bidding an unmakeable one; they may bid game or slam in the wrong suit. And you can cause all this confusion to the enemy with very little risk if you pre-empt with the right type of hand.

The right type of hand is *worthless on defense*. A hand like

♠ A Q 10 x x x   ♡ Q 10 x   ◇ J 10 x   ♣ none

is *not* in the pre-emptive pattern despite the long, strong suit; you might take a big set and find that the opponents couldn't make any contract of their own. But a hand like

♠ Q J 10 x x x   ♡ x   ◇ x x   ♣ 10 x x

although much weaker, is a safer pre-empt, for whenever you go down enough to hurt, the opponents could have made a game or slam. You will have lost nothing.

Your *defensive* strength, then, determines *whether or not* you pre-empt when you have a long suit. Your *offensive* strength controls the *level* at which you pre-empt.

The most common high pre-emptive bids are the opening 3-bids in a suit. Three-bids are made on hands with virtually no defense and 5 or 6 playing tricks. They are *hopeless* hands; opener has no thought of game unless partner has a powerhouse.

With ♠ Q J 10 x x x x ♥ x ♦ x x ♣ 10 x x
open 3 ♠.

With ♠ x x ♥ x ♦ K Q J x x x ♣ J x x x
open 3 ♦.

With ♠ x ♥ x x ♦ Q J x ♣ A 10 9 x x x x
pass. You have too much defense to pre-empt.

When you hold a hand of true pre-emptive pattern but more than 6 winners, you dare not open with a 3-bid for fear of missing game. With a long major suit, no defense, and some hope of making game, open with a game bid— 4 ♥ or 4 ♠. If partner has a strong hand or good fitting cards you'll make your contract; if he hasn't, you'll be taking a good sacrifice.

With ♠ K Q J x x x x ♥ x x ♦ x x ♣ x
open 4 ♠.

With ♠ x x ♥ Q J 10 x x x ♦ Q J 10 x ♣ none
open 4 ♥.

In minor suits it is much the same. If you have the right type of hand, 5 or 6 winners, make a 3-bid; 7 or 8 winners, a 4-bid (4 ♣, 4 ♦). You also have available the rare opening bids of 5 ♣ and 5 ♦ for very strong playing hands.

Responding to Pre-empts

Responder will normally pass over any of these pre-emptive openings, but occasionally his hand will call for a bid because of its strength *or its weakness*. To raise to game after a 3 ♥ or 3 ♠ opening bid, responder must be able to furnish 4 to 5 taking tricks, as opener has only 5 or

6 winners himself. These "taking tricks" must be either Quick Tricks or ruffing tricks—point count is not a reliable guide, for isolated queens and jacks are worthless facing a pre-emptive hand.

Ruffing tricks may be relied on only if you have at least three-card trump support. If you have enough trumps to ruff with, figure on one trick for a singleton, two tricks for a void. Add these to your Quick Trick valuation, and a total of 4 tricks means that you *may* raise; a total of 5 means that you *must*.

♠ K x x   ♥ x x   ♦ A Q x x   ♣ A K x x

If partner opens 3 ♠, bid 4 ♠. You have 4 Quick Tricks.

♠ K x x   ♥ A K J x x   ♦ K x x x   ♣ x

If partner opens 3 ♠, bid 4 ♠. You have 3 Quick Tricks plus one ruffing trick.

♠ K x x   ♥ K Q J x x   ♦ Q J x   ♣ A x

If partner opens 3 ♠, pass. For all your 16 points, you have only 2½ tricks.

Take a typical 3 ♠ opening—

♠ Q J 10 x x x x   ♥ x   ♦ x x   ♣ x x x

and see how many tricks must be lost opposite each of the example hands.

You should also bid over partner's pre-emptive opening when you have a fit for his suit and a weak hand defensively. Suppose partner opens 3 ♦, your right-hand opponent passes, and you hold

♠ A x x   ♥ x x   ♦ K J x x   ♣ K x x x

Bid 5 ♦! You won't make the contract, but your opponents surely can score a major-suit game, and possibly even a slam. Don't give them bidding room in which to exchange information.

Suppose partner opens 3 ♠, your right-hand opponent passes, and you hold:

♠ K x x x   ♥ x x   ♦ A Q x x x   ♣ x x

Bid 4 ♠. You can't make your contract, but the opponents can make theirs if you let them find out what it is.

The general principle is this: when your partner pre-empts and you intend to sacrifice over an enemy game contract, *make the bid right away*. Never stick your head into the sand and pass, hoping that the game the opponents can make will disappear. If you wait until the enemy bids its game before taking your sacrifice, you give them a "fielder's choice." First you let them exchange information, then you give them the opportunity either to double you or to bid more themselves. Instead, you should *bid at once as high as you are willing to go*.

Suppose partner opens 3 ♠, your right-hand opponent doubles, and it's up to you with

♠ Qxxxx   ♡ Ax   ◇ Axxx   ♣ xx

What do you bid? Well, how high are you willing to go? The opponents can surely make 5 ♡ and you can't be hurt much at 5 ♠, so that's the answer. 5 ♠ is how high you are willing to go, so bid it right away. Here is the complete hand:

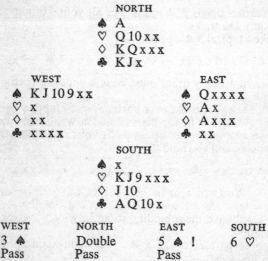

NORTH
♠ A
♡ Q 10 x x
◇ K Q x x x
♣ K J x

WEST
♠ K J 10 9 x x
♡ x
◇ x x
♣ x x x x

EAST
♠ Q x x x
♡ A x
◇ A x x x
♣ x x

SOUTH
♠ x
♡ K J 9 x x x
◇ J 10
♣ A Q 10 x

WEST	NORTH	EAST	SOUTH
3 ♠	Double	5 ♠ !	6 ♡
Pass	Pass	Pass	

South's bid was perfectly reasonable—he had a very strong hand and no room at all for investigation. The 5 ♠ bid crowded him into bidding an unmakeable slam. Note that any lower bid by East would let North-South discover that they were off two aces. Then if East sacrificed at 5 ♠, he would be doubled and would take a loss instead of a profit.

Notice, too, West's pass over 6 ♡. This respected another general principle: *when you have pre-empted, your partner, not you, must do all further sacrifice bidding.* West had no defense against 6 ♡, but he had already annnounced this with his 3 ♠ bid. From then on, East assumed full control.

In all this discussion of pre-emptive bidding, nothing at all has been said about vulnerability. Actually, vulnerability conditions do not affect pre-empts so much as you might imagine. On the surface, it would appear that it is when the opponents are vulnerable and you are not that you should pre-empt most freely. But the lower scale of penalties that you pay to stop a 700-point rubber is offset by the greater likelihood that the opponents will win the rubber anyway, after your "successful" sacrifice. Mathematically, the most favorable vulnerability for pre-emptives is both vulnerable, for if the opponents accept a penalty instead of scoring their second game, you have as much chance of winning the rubber as they do. The real concession you make to vulnerability comes when you are vulnerable and the opponents are not. Under these conditions, do not pre-empt at all. The odds are much too unfavorable.

Weak 2-Bids

The Weak 2-Bids—opening bids of 2 ◊, 2 ♡, 2 ♠— differ in one fundamental respect from the pre-emptive bids already discussed. Those are all "tactical" bids, intended not to enable the partnership to arrive at its best contract, but to prevent the opponents from arriving at theirs. The weak 2-bids are *descriptive,* not *tactical.* They promise specific values, both offensive and defensive, and are intended as much to help your side get to its top spot as to impede the enemy.

A hand must meet two sets of requirements to qualify as a weak 2-bid.

1. STRENGTH. The strength must be just under that of an opening bid—9 to 11 points including distribution, and the hand must contain no more and no less than 1½ to 2 Quick Tricks.

2. SUIT. The suit must be exactly 6 cards long, and

it must be semisolid; that is, playable opposite a singleton in partner's hand. As you can see from these requirements, the weak 2-bid is really a light opening bid with a strong suit. For example:

♠ KQJxxx   ♡ Kxx   ◊ xx   ♣ xx

This is a typical opening 2 ♠ bid. You would just as soon keep the opponents out of the auction, but if they bid, partner can count on you for a trick or two in defense.

Your strong suit gives you protection two ways. First, the opponents will not get rich doubling you. (You have to worry about this more with weak 2-bids than with higher pre-empts, for your defensive strength, combined with a smattering of cards in partner's hand, may be enough to prevent the opponents from making game.) Second, you almost surely do not have a better suit in which to play the hand. (The weak 2-bid makes it difficult to find a fit in another suit, particularly under the game level, so if you open a 2-bid in a weak suit you may take a loss when you should be making a profit at some other trump declaration.)

♠ xx   ♡ xx   ◊ AKJ10xx   ♣ xxx

Open 2 ◊. You have 9 points (counting 1 point for the six-card suit), 2 Quick Tricks, and a fine, solid suit.

♠ A10xxxx   ♡ KQx   ◊ xxx   ♣ x

Pass. You have 11 points, 2 Quick Tricks, and a six-card suit, but your suit is not solid enough either to avert a disastrous penalty or to be sure you want to play with spades as trumps. Your hand would make a fine dummy for a heart or diamond contract.

♠ xx   ♡ AJ109xx   ◊ Kxx   ♣ xx

Open 2 ♡. Now you have 9 points, not 11 points, but your suit is strong enough.

♠ xx   ♡ AQJxxx   ◊ x   ♣ Kxxx

Open 1 ♡ not 2 ♡. Adding 1 point each for the six-card suit and the singleton, you have 12 points. So you are strong enough for a one-bid, too strong for a two-bid.

Responding to the Weak 2-Bid

When your partner opens with a weak 2-bid, you know just about all there is to know about his hand. You, the responder, must make all the decisions for the partnership. You may decide that you are in the best spot, and pass. You may decide that the opponents can make a high contract, and raise opener's suit pre-emptively. You may decide that you have a game, and bid it.

To raise a 2 ♡ or 2 ♠ opening bid to four, just as to raise a 3-bid to game, responder needs *tricks* not points. You will have to provide about four winners in Quick Tricks or in ruffing tricks. Suppose your partner opens 2 ♠ and you hold

    ♠ xxx   ♡ xx   ◊ AQxx   ♣ AKxx

Bid 4 ♠. You have 3½ Quick Tricks, and your doubleton might be worth something.

    ♠ Axx   ♡ QJx   ◊ QJx   ♣ KJxx

Pass. You have 14 points but not nearly enough tricks.

    ♠ Axxx   ♡ x   ◊ AQxx   ♣ xxxx

Bid 4 ♠. You will furnish 2½ Quick Tricks and either one or two ruffing tricks, according to whether partner has two hearts or three.

    ♠ xx   ♡ x   ◊ AKxxx   ♣ Axxxx

Pass. You have 3 Quick Tricks, but your singleton is valueless with only two trumps.

Take the typical 2 ♠ bid we cited earlier:

    ♠ KQJxxx   ♡ Kxx   ◊ xx   ♣ xx

and see what sort of play you have for 4 ♠ facing each of the example hands we have given responder.

When responder has a fit in opener's suit but a weak hand, he raises pre-emptively, just as he would opposite a 3-bid. Of course, he must bear in mind that the opening 2-bid, unlike a 3-bid, contains some defensive strength. He must not be too quick to assume that the enemy can make game. But the basic theory of all pre-emptive bidding applies: *if you are going to sacrifice, do it right away*.

Partner opens 2 ♠, right-hand opponent passes, you hold:

    ♠ A 10 xx   ♡ x   ◊ xx   ♣ Jxxxx

Bid 4 ♠. Leave as little room as possible for the opponents to find their best spot.

Partner opens 2 ◊, your right-hand opponent doubles for takeout, you hold:

♠ xx   ♡ x   ◊ Jxxxx   ♣ A10xxx

Bid 5 ◊. You intend to sacrifice over 4 ♡ or 4 ♠. Do it *at once* for maximum effect.

Partner opens 2 ♠, your right-hand opponent passes, you hold:

♠ Qxx   ♡ KQ10x   ◊ Kxxx   ♣ xx

Bid 3 ♠. You are not inviting partner to bid game—he has already told you exactly how strong his hand is, so *you* must make all such decisions. What you are doing is to *bid at once as high as you are willing to go*. If the opponents contest the auction, make them do it at a level at which you think you can set them.

The raise of opener's suit (Opener: 2 ♡; Responder: 3 ♡) is pre-emptive, but it is possible for responder to get a little more information about opener's hand in other ways. He can, for example, bid 2 NT (Opener: 2 ♠; Responder: 2 NT). This asks opener to bid the suit in which he has outside strength.

♠ AJ109xx	♠ KQx
♡ xxx	♡ AKxx
◊ Kx	◊ Jxx
♣ xx	♣ Axx

OPENER	RESPONDER
2 ♠	2 NT
3 ◊	3 NT

Responder, with 4 QT, wants to be in game but is not sure whether to play in 3 NT or 4 ♠. Using the forcing bid of 2 NT, he learns that opener has some diamond strength and so can bid the safer 3 NT game. Had opener rebid 3 ♣ over 2 NT, responder would have contracted for 4. ♠

Any new suit bid by responder is a one-round force on the opening bidder. Responder will use these bids on the rare occasions when he is interested in playing with some suit of his own as trumps. Opener will raise responder's suit if he has some support for it, otherwise he will rebid his own suit.

♠ A J 10 9 x x	♠ x
♡ x x x	♡ A K J x x x
◇ K x	◇ A x
♣ x x	♣ K x x x

OPENER	RESPONDER
2 ♠	3 ♡
4 ♡	Pass

Responder does not have the values to bid game in spades, but wants to play 4 ♡ if opener has some tolerance for that contract. Had opener rebid 3 ♠, responder would have passed.

Everything said so far about requirements for weak 2-bids and responses to them applies only to first and second hand bids, made before partner has passed. As you will see in the next section, third and fourth hand weak 2-bids may be quite unorthodox and require separate treatment.

THIRD- AND FOURTH-HAND OPENINGS

All authorities on "standard bidding" will tell you to make shaded, substandard opening bids in third position. The theory behind this is that when your partner has passed originally you can drop his first response no matter what it is; thus you can afford to open light, for you can keep the auction low. For instance:

FIRST HAND	THIRD HAND
Pass	1 ♠
2 ♣	Pass

These same authorities, going further, tell responder that he can afford to make strong-sounding bids—to bid new suits at the two-level, to jump to 2 NT, to jump in opener's suit—with less strength when he has passed originally. Here again the theory is that these strong responses do not force the partnership to a high contract (as they would if responder were not a passed hand) for opener can pass them.

This theory is attractive, for it lets both partners bid a lot, and every one loves to bid. But it has a serious flaw. This flaw is *not* that a light third-hand opening facing a shaded response may lead to trouble. Consider this auction:

```
       ♠ xx                    ♠ AQJxx
       ♡ KJxxxx                ♡ xx
       ◇ xx                    ◇ QJxx
       ♣ Q10x                  ♣ xx

    FIRST HAND               THIRD HAND
       Pass                     1 ♠
       2 ♡                      Pass
```

The two-heart contract is risky, but unlikely to be
doubled and penalized severely. This sort of auction makes
it difficult for the enemy to reach their best contract, and
illustrates not the disadvantage but the advantage of light
third-hand bidding.

The trouble comes, strangely enough, when the third
hand opening bidder has a perfectly sound hand which he
would open in any position, and when responder, first hand,
has a normal strong response. Routine, everyday auctions
are made complicated when responder must suspect that
opener hasn't really got his bid, when opener must allow
for a shaded response. A partnership considered by many
to be the very best in the world missed a vulnerable game
in a World Championship match because of this:

```
       ♠ x                     ♠ K10xxx
       ♡ AKQxxx                ♡ Jxx
       ◇ xxxx                  ◇ Kx
       ♣ xx                    ♣ AQ10

    FIRST HAND               THIRD HAND
       Pass                     1 ♠
       2 ♡                      Pass
```

Had the opening bidder been in first or second seat, four
hearts would have been reached automatically. But the
third-hand opening led each partner to fear that the other
had shaded his bid.

Another unfortunate feature of light third-hand openings
is that any bid that responder makes may become the final
contract. Thus responder cannot make any temporizing
bids; he must walk constantly in the shadow of the sudden-
death pass from opener. Suppose you hold

```
       ♠ xxx    ♡ Kx    ◇ AJxx    ♣ Kxxx
```

and the auction goes

YOU	PARTNER
Pass	1 ♡

What do you respond? Do you bid 2 NT and risk playing this contract with 20 points and no spade stopper in the combined hands, if partner holds a light third-hand bid like

♠ xx   ♡ AQJxx   ◇ Q 10 xx   ♣ xx?

Do you bid 2 ♣, and play this contract with K x x x opposite two small trumps if partner has the same light bid? Or do you respond 1 NT, and miss a lay-down game when partner has a sound minimum like

♠ QJx   ♡ AQJxx   ◇ KQx   ♣ xx

for his third-hand bid?

Standard bidders have tried very hard to solve this type of problem. Some come to an agreement with their partners that the 1 NT response (1 ♠—1 NT) and the single raise (1 ♠—2 ♠) may be made on good hands after an original pass. Some have adopted an artificial response which asks opener if he has a legitimate opening bid. Most just scramble along as well as they can. But all eventually come to grief. It is impossible to bid safely or accurately when the opening bid and response have such poorly defined, hazy limits.

Our solution is simply to have the opening bid mean what it says regardless of the position of the opener. The requirements for an opening bid of 1 ♣, 1 ◇, 1 ♡ or 1 ♠ are the same in third hand as in first. The responses are the same. Opener's rebids are the same. (For example, if opener bids 1 ♠, he will not pass a 2 ♣ response whether or not responder has passed originally.) We have devoted a lot of effort to make our System as accurate as possible, and we refuse to throw it all away for the pre-emptive value of the light third-hand opening bid.

Not that we have to pass meekly in third seat and give the opponents all the room they want to find their best contract. When we want to open light in third seat, we have available the weak notrump for balanced hands and the weak 2-bids for unbalanced hands. Note that these are *high* bids, which give us really effective pre-emption, using up a lot of the enemy's bidding space. And they are *limited* bids, which serve to warn partner at once that we do not expect to have a game opposite his passed hand.

The weak 2-bid changes in character when used facing a passed hand. In first or second seat, before partner has passed, you use two-bids to tell partner what sort of hand you hold. This *descriptive* use is rare, for you must wait until you have exactly the right hand for it—a semisolid six-card suit, 1½ to 2 QT, too few points for a one-bid. However, once partner has passed, these rigid requirements do not apply, for your purpose has changed. Now you are not trying to describe your hand to partner, who is pretty surely going to pass no matter what you have. You are trying to impede the opponents.

Two-bids are opened in third seat, as in first or second, with the perfect "book" hands, but you open two-bids with many other hands as well—with most of the hands, in fact, which are opened with light third-hand one-bids in standard bidding.

♠ KJxxxx   ♡ xx   ◇ A10xx   ♣ x

Open 2 ♠ in third position. First hand, you would pass because your suit is too ragged; you would fear that the hand might play better in a different suit. But once partner has passed, your concern is to buy the hand cheap or to interrupt the opponents' communications, not to find your own maximum contract.

♠ AJ10xx   ♡ xx   ◇ x   ♣ Q10xxx

Open 2 ♠ in third position. This would be an unthinkable bid in first or second seat, completely misdescribing your hand to partner. But once you know partner has no opening bid, you are worried not about him, but about the opponents.

♠ xx   ♡ AQJ10xx   ◇ Kxx   ♣ xx

Open 2 ♡ in any position (even as fourth hand after three passes).

Here is how we would handle the problem hand discussed earlier in this section:

♠ xxx	♠ xx
♡ Kx	♡ AQJxx
◇ AJxx	◇ Q10xx
♣ Kxxx	♣ xx

FIRST HAND	THIRD HAND
Pass	2 ♡
Pass	

After a third-hand weak 2-bid, responder passes without a problem. He knows that no game can be made.

Actually, it is very unusual for responder to bid over a third-hand weak 2-bid. If responder does act, any bid he makes has its natural meaning and can be passed by opener. The auction

FIRST HAND	THIRD HAND
Pass	2 ♠
3 ♣	

means that responder wants to play the contract of three clubs. He may have a hand like

♠ x   ♡ xx   ◇ Kxx   ♣ KQ 10 xxxx

With this hand he would pass over a first- or second-hand 2 ♠ opening, knowing opener's spade suit to be playable opposite a singleton. A 3 ♣ bid would then be a forcing game try, not an attempt to escape from spades. However, the third hand 2 ♠ opening can be made on a ragged suit, so responder runs out to 3 ♣, trying for a plus score, not for a game.

The raise of the weak 2-bid also changes in meaning when responder has passed originally. Opposite a first or second hand bid, the raise is pre-emptive, for there is no need for responder to ask opener "How good is your 2-bid?" when the 2-bid has such rigid requirements. But the third-hand weak 2-bid is not rigidly limited—it has a wide range. So the raise becomes a game invitation; responder wants to be in game if opener has an upper-level bid. For example:

♠ Qxxxx	♠ x
♡ KJxx	♡ Q 10 xxxx
◇ x	◇ AKxx
♣ Axx	♣ xx

FIRST HAND	THIRD HAND
Pass	2 ♡
3 ♡	4 ♡

The weak notrump does not change radically when used in third position. It is true that if you elect to open a light balanced hand after partner has passed, you must open it with 1 NT even if your point-count is lower than the required 12 points. But you are making a highly questionable decision when you open a subminimum weak notrump opposite a passed hand. The risk is normally too great.

One requirement that you can ignore in third seat is the Quick Trick minimum. Once partner has passed, you can open with 1 NT on

♠ Q J x   ♡ K J x   ♢ K J x x   ♣ Q x x

You no longer have to fear that partner will take some violent action—a jump to a suit game, a penalty double of an enemy overcall—which your high-card structure cannot support.

You will notice that nowhere in this section are rules set down for when to open a light third-hand weak 2-bid or weak NT, and when not to. There aren't any such rules. These are tactical bids, not descriptive bids. Your use of them must depend on your estimate of the bidding habits of your opponents, on the vulnerability, on the mood and mien and climate at the table.

But there is one hard and fast rule: *Never open with a one-bid in a suit without the normal requirements. If you open light, open with a weak 2-bid or a weak notrump.* If you don't have the material for a one-bid, if you are too weak for a weak notrump, if you have no suit in which you care to open a weak 2-bid, don't despair. You are, after all, allowed to pass in third position.

PSYCHIC OPENING BIDS

No treatment of opening bids would be complete without some discussion of bluff openings on very bad hands—"psychic" bids. For psychics can be very effective weapons. Not that they are likely to frighten the opponents out of entering the auction; when you have a miserably weak hand, the enemy will surely have more than enough strength to act over your "opening bid." But psychic openings do work for you.

What they do is to jostle the opponents out of their normal, accustomed auctions into strange and uncomfortable situations. Everyone knows how to conduct the bidding of a strong hand when his partner opens the auction;

but no one is used to holding a powerful hand when an opponent opens the bidding and partner overcalls or makes a takeout double. Here is a hand from a recent team championship:

```
                        NORTH
                     ♠ x x x
                     ♡ Q
                     ◇ K x x x
                     ♣ K Q 10 x x

        WEST                          EAST
     ♠ A J 10 x x                  ♠ K Q x
     ♡ K x x x                     ♡ A J 10 x x x
     ◇ A x                         ◇ x x
     ♣ A x                         ♣ x x

                        SOUTH
                     ♠ x x
                     ♡ x x
                     ◇ Q J 10 x x
                     ♣ J x x x
```

SOUTH	WEST	NORTH	EAST
Pass	1 ♠	Pass	2 ♡
Pass	4 ♡	Pass	4 NT
Pass	5 ♠	Pass	5 NT
Pass	6 ◇	Pass	7 ♡
Pass	Pass	Pass	

This bidding occurred when our team mates held the East-West cards. Their auction was smooth and easy. At the end of it, East could count thirteen tricks—five tricks in spades, for West's opening showed a five-card suit; six tricks in hearts, for West's jump to 4 ♡ meant that the suit was solid; two tricks more in aces, shown by the Blackwood Convention. So the grand slam was bid and made.

However, when our opponents bid the East-West cards against us, they did not have such an easy time. This was the auction:

SOUTH	WEST	NORTH	EAST
1 ◇ !	Double	Redouble	2 ♡
Pass	4 ♡	Pass	Pass
Pass			

They were not fooled by the psychic. Everyone at the table knew that South could not have a real opening bid with all the other players showing strong hands. But the psychic bid distorted our opponents' normal auction. West never got to bid his spade suit, so East couldn't realize the power of his spade support. They had no specific understanding of what East showed by his jump to 2 ♡ or of what West needed for his jump to 4 ♡. (East thought that West was just making sure he reached game; West thought that East might have less for his jump to 2 ♡.)

Of course, it is perfectly possible to bid a small slam or even a grand slam on these cards after a psychic 1 ◊ opening. But it is much more difficult, for normal bidding methods are not designed for slam investigation after the opponents open the auction.

The price for disturbing the enemy's bidding on their big hands is not paid in disastrous sets when the psychic "goes wrong." Strangely, the psychic opening is one of the safest of all unorthodox bids. Almost invariably, the opponent who sits behind the psychic bidder doubles for takeout or overcalls and the psychic bidder is out of trouble unless his partner gets too active. But his partner is alert to the possibility of a psychic opening and will tread warily.

And here is where you pay for psychic bidding—in the "treading warily," in the loss of partnership confidence on the hand when you haven't psyched but partner fears you have. This is a heavy price. It is far better never to psyche at all than to allow the fear of the psychic to undermine your whole bidding structure.

But we have our cake and eat it too—we psyche occasionally and still retain partnership confidence. This we do by making the bluff opening a disciplined bid, promising specific values; by making it a *descriptive* as well as a tactical bid. There are three requirements:

1. A biddable suit, at least four cards long and usually five cards long, headed by the ace, king, or queen.
2. 3 to 6 points in high cards.
3. No ace or king in a side suit.

Here are a few typical psychic opening bids:

♠	x x	♡	K J x x x	◊	x x x	♣	x x x	Open 1 ♡
♠	x x	♡	x x x	◊	J x x	♣	Q 10 9 x x	Open 1 ♣
♠	x x x	♡	x x x	◊	K Q J x	♣	x x x	Open 1 ◊

However, these next hands may not be opened with psychics:

♠ x x x ♡ K x x ◇ Q J 10 x x ♣ x x—because it has a side king.

♠ x x ♡ A Q J x x ◇ x x x x ♣ x x—because it is too strong.

♠ x x ♡ x x x ◇ J x x ♣ J 10 9 x x—because it is too weak, and because the club suit has no high honor.

This "disciplined" psychic preserves partnership confidence in two ways. First, it tells partner exactly what sort of hand to expect if you turn out to be psyching. Second, it allows partner to bid normally when he fears you do not have a legitimate opening bid, even if his normal response is a jump raise in your suit. For example, if you open 1 ♠ and partner holds

♠ A K x x ♡ x x ◇ K Q x x ♣ x x x

he can jump to 3 ♠ not caring whether you have opened with

1. ♠ Q J 10 x x ♡ A x x ◇ x x ♣ A Q x
or
2. ♠ Q J 10 x x ♡ x x x ◇ x x ♣ x x x

In the first case, you will bid and probably make 4 ♠. In the second, you are down two at 3 ♠, but the opponents surely can make game at hearts. In either case, partner's 3 ♠ bid is safe and sound.

A side advantage to this type of psychic opening is that it tells partner what to lead in the likely event that the opponents buy the contract. In the very nature of the requirements for the psychic, you can stand the lead of the suit you open and of no other suit.

Another secondary advantage is that responder, holding a very strong hand, can tell almost surely whether he can make a game facing a "disciplined" psychic opening. Suppose you hold:

♠ x x ♡ A x x ◇ A K 10 x x ♣ A K x

and partner opens 1 ♠. You have a shrewd idea that he is psyching, but you make your normal 2 ◇ response. If he doesn't have an opening bid he will pass this "forcing bid," and you will be in a reasonable contract. But suppose he opens 1 ♠ and you hold:

♠ A Q x   ♡ A K Q J x x   ◇ K x   ♣ x x

Now you can make game even if partner has opened a psychic, for then he must have the ♠ K. So you cannot bid 2 ♡ and allow opener to pass if he has a psychic opening bid.

For these hands you have available the jump shift—responder's jump in a new suit (1 ♠—3 ♡; 1 ♣—2 ◇). The jump shift is forcing on the opening bidder *even if he is psyching*. In fact, the primary message of this jump shift is the question: "Partner, do you have a legitimate or a psychic opening bid?"

Opener answers, "I am psyching," by making the lowest possible bid in no trump or in his original suit, whichever is cheaper. (This minimum rebid will always be 2 NT or three of the original suit; it will never be two of a suit or 3 NT.)

All these auctions show psychic opening bids:

OPENER	RESPONDER
1 ♠	3 ♡
3 ♠	
1 ◇	3 ♣
3 ◇	
1 ◇	2 ♠
2 NT	
1 ♣	2 ◇
2 NT	

Opener answers, "I have a real opening bid," by making any other bid. All these sequences confirm a standard opening, for opener did not make the cheapest sign-off bid:

OPENER	RESPONDER
1 ◇	2 ♡
2 ♠	
1 ♠	3 ♡
3 NT	

	OPENER	RESPONDER
	1 ♣	2 ♡
	3 ♣	

———————

| | 1 ♡ | 2 ♠ |
| | 3 ♠ | |

Let's see how this works.

OPENER	RESPONDER
♠ K 10 x x x	♠ A Q x
♡ x x	♡ A K Q J x x
◇ x x x	◇ K x
♣ x x x	♣ x x

OPENER	RESPONDER
1 ♠	3 ♡
3 ♠	4 ♡
Pass	

A classic auction! Opener has an ideal "disciplined" psychic. Responder wants to be in game facing a psychic, so he uses the jump shift to ask partner about his opening. Opener's 3 ♠ rebid states definitely that the opening is psychic, so responder settles for game. Over any other rebid, responder would have used the Blackwood Convention to check for aces, and would have bid a small or grand slam accordingly.

Note that without the "descriptive" psychic opening bid, the final contract might well have been 1 ♡, not 4 ♡.

VARIATION

Opening Bid of 3 NT: Instead of showing 27 or 28 points in high cards, the opening bid of 3 NT may be made on a hand of 20 to 23 points with a long minor suit that will produce five or six very fast tricks.

♠ K x   ♡ A x   ◇ A K Q x x x   ♣ K Q x

Open 3 NT. You have the points for 2 NT, but the *tricks* for 3 NT.

When this meaning is assigned to the opening bid of 3 NT, responder needs about 10 points (including at least one ace) to suggest a slam.

Getting out of 2 NT: Responder can get out of 2 NT and still stay out of game by responding 3 ◊. This directs opener to bid 3 ♡.

Responder will pass 3 ♡ or bid his true suit. In either case, responder shows a six-card suit and a worthless hand.

♠ xx   ♡ Jxxxxx   ◊ xx   ♣ xxx

Bid 3 ◊ in response to an opening bid of 2 NT. Opener will bid 3 ♡, and you will pass. You will probably be two or more tricks better off at hearts than at notrump. (If your long suit were spades, you would bid 3 ◊ first, forcing the 3 ♡ rebid by opener; and then you would bid 3 ♠.)

Chapter 3

After a Major-Suit Opening Bid

AN OPENING BID of one spade or one heart provides a very solid foundation to the rest of the auction. Remember, the major-suit opening bid is made only with a five-card or longer suit. You never need flounder about to find a trump suit; should no fit be found in a second suit, you almost always have a "home" at the two-level in opener's major. This means that much of the bidding effort you ordinarily expend on *What should be trump?* can be devoted to *How high shall we go?*

THE 1 NT RESPONSE

The most important tool in this investigation is the 1 NT response. This is *artificial* and *forcing*. That is to say, when the auction proceeds:

OPENER	RESPONDER
1 ♠	1 NT

this 1 NT response means "Partner, I haven't got a very powerful hand, so whether we have a game or not depends on the quality of your opening bid. I'll let you know in a minute just how interested I am in going to game and where this interest lies."

It definitely does *not* mean, "Partner, I want to play this hand in 1 NT." In fact, the hand cannot play in 1 NT, for the opening bidder *must bid again over this response.*

Although you cannot play a hand at 1 NT after an opening bid of one spade, you will find that this inability costs you nothing of real value. The theory is this: if responder has at least two or more spades, a contract of two spades is preferable to 1 NT, since opener has at least a five-card suit. If responder has a singleton spade, the hand should probably play not in notrump but in clubs, diamonds, or hearts.

Obviously, then, opener will rebid his suit over 1 NT

only if he is willing to play opposite a singleton—that is, if he has a six-card suit. Otherwise he bids a lower-ranking suit. And if he has no lower-ranking four-card suit? The opener then rebids in his lower three-card suit. For example:

		OPENER	RESPONDER
♠	K x x	1 ♡	1 NT
♡	A Q 10 x x	2 ◇	
◇	K x x		
♣	J x		

The heart suit isn't long enough to rebid over 1 NT. Opener may not pass 1 NT, so must bid a short minor suit. Since he holds only two clubs, he bids 2 ◇.

		OPENER	RESPONDER
♠	A J x x x	1 ♠	1 NT
♡	K x	2 ♣	
◇	A J x		
♣	Q x x		

Here again opener cannot rebid his suit and must bid a three-card minor. With equal length, he chooses clubs, the lower-ranking suit.

		OPENER	RESPONDER
♠	A K J x x	1 ♠	1 NT
♡	Q x x x	2 ♡	
◇	K x x		
♣	x		

Opener prefers to bid his four-card heart suit, rather than a three-card minor.

		OPENER	RESPONDER
♠	A Q 10 x x x	1 ♠	1 NT
♡	x	2 ♠	
◇	K x x		
♣	K x x		

With a six-card suit, opener may rebid his spades.

The initial bid of 1 NT by responder covers a very wide range of hands, from 5 points to 11 points, from 4-3-3-3 distribution up to freaks. Therefore, responder's second bid is very important, for it will clarify his holding. On this standard auction

OPENER	RESPONDER
1 ♠	1 NT
2 ♣	?

responder has five different types of rebid available. The basic one goes

OPENER	RESPONDER
1 ♠	1 NT
2 ♣	2 ♠

This sequence describes a hand of no particular merit —not strong, for a thin 9 points is the absolute top limit; with no long suit, for this would be the occasion to bid it; without real spade support, for with three or more trumps responder would have raised spades directly. Thus, opener must be very strong (at least 17 points) to go further, for responder has a featureless hand without a good fit. Here is a typical auction:

♠ K Q 10 x x	♠ J x
♡ x x	♡ 10 9 x x
◇ A Q x	◇ K J x x
♣ J x x	♣ Q x x

OPENER	RESPONDER
1 ♠	1 NT
2 ♣	2 ♠
Pass	

Give opening bidder another ace

♠ K Q 10 x x   ♡ A x   ◇ A Q x   ♣ J x x

and he would still pass two spades. But make his hand a little better still

♠ A Q 10 x x   ♡ A x   ◇ A Q x   ♣ J x x

and opener would try 2 NT over responder's two-spade rebid.

As you vary responder's hand, giving it more body or more shape, his rebid varies also. If he has a six-card suit or a strong five-card suit, he bids it here:

OPENER	RESPONDER
1 ♠	1 NT
2 ♣	2 ♡

This auction also is frequently passed out at this point, for although responder has a good suit, he has a weakish hand and no great fit with either suit bid by opener. Still, opener should make a try for game if he has more than a minimum bid plus a fit in responder's suit. Here are two examples:

♠ K Q 10 x x	♠ x x
♡ x x	♡ A J x x x x
◊ A Q x	◊ x x
♣ J x x	♣ Q x x

OPENER	RESPONDER
1 ♠	1 NT
2 ♣	2 ♡
Pass	

Responder shows a good suit but a bad hand, and opener, with a minimum, passes. How else would you get to two hearts?

♠ K Q 10 x x	♠ x
♡ A x	♡ K x x
◊ A Q x	◊ K J x x x x
♣ J x x	♣ Q x x

OPENER	RESPONDER
1 ♠	1 NT
2 ♣	2 ◊
3 ◊	3 NT
Pass	

Again, responder shows a limited hand with a long suit. This time, though, opener has a solid opening with a fit with responder, so he raises. Responder, with a *good* bad hand, bids game. Without the king of hearts he would pass three diamonds. Opener, without the ace of hearts, would pass two diamonds.

When responder wants to play in opener's secondary suit, he can pass or raise, depending on his strength. (A good 8 points is a minimum raise.) Of course, he must bear in mind the possibility that opener has bid a *three*-card minor. If responder raises a minor, it is almost surely with five-card support.

♠ K Q 10 x x	♠ x
♡ x x	♡ 10 9 x x
◊ A Q x	◊ K J x
♣ J x x	♣ K Q x x x

OPENER	RESPONDER
1 ♠	1 NT
2 ♣	3 ♣
Pass	

Responder, with five clubs and 9 high-card points, has a sound raise to three clubs. Opener, with a bare minimum, passes.

♠ K Q 10 x x	♠ x
♡ A x	♡ 10 9 x x
◇ A Q x	◇ K J x
♣ J x x	♣ K Q x x x

OPENER	RESPONDER
1 ♠	1 NT
2 ♣	3 ♣
3 NT	Pass

Here, opener, with extra values over his opening, goes on to game.

To pass two clubs on this sequence, responder does not need such fine support. Any time he has a poor hand with a singleton in opener's suit and no long suit of his *own*, this will be his action.

♠ K Q 10 x x	♠ x
♡ x x	♡ 10 9 x x
◇ A Q x	◇ K J x x
♣ J x x	♣ Q x x x

OPENER	RESPONDER
1 ♠	1 NT
2 ♣	Pass

Responder has no reason to go further. The final contract of two clubs is not gilt-edged, but no contract is likely to make.

Responder's most constructive rebid is 2 NT. With the sequence

OPENER	RESPONDER
1 ♠	1 NT
2 ♣	2 NT

he describes a hand of about 10 points. (It might be a robust 9 points or a scrawny 11 points.) He doesn't have a fit for spades, but he is interested in game on straight power. If opener has about 16 points, there should be a reasonable play for 3 NT; if not, 2 NT is probably safe. For example:

♠ KQ10xx	♠ Jx
♡ xx	♡ K109x
♢ AQx	♢ KJxx
♣ Jxx	♣ Qxx

OPENER	RESPONDER
1 ♠	1 NT
2 ♣	2 NT
Pass	

Responder's 10 points is enough for a game try, but opener, with a minimum, passes.

♠ KQ10xx	♠ Jx
♡ Ax	♡ K109x
♢ AQx	♢ KJxx
♣ Jxx	♣ Qxx

OPENER	RESPONDER
1 ♠	1 NT
2 ♣	2 NT
3 NT	Pass

Now opener has the values to accept the invitation and bids 3 NT.

In all these auctions, opener has bid two clubs over 1 NT. Let's see what happens when opener has a six-card suit and rebids it:

OPENER	RESPONDER
1 ♠	1 NT
2 ♠	?

When responder has any of the bad hands for his 1 NT response, he passes. There can be no reason to disturb the contract except to try for game. So responder passes with

♠ Jx	♡ 109xx	♢ KJxx	♣ Qxx
♠ xx	♡ AJxxxx	♢ xx	♣ Qxx
♠ x	♡ 109xx	♢ KJxx	♣ Qxxx

or even with

♠ x   ♥ 109xx   ♦ KJx   ♣ KQxxx

If responder bids a new suit at the three-level

OPENER	RESPONDER
1 ♠	1 NT
2 ♠	3 ♦

he wants to go to game if opener has a fit and some extra value. For instance:

♠ KQ10xxx	♠ x
♥ Ax	♥ Kxx
♦ AQx	♦ KJxxxx
♣ J·x	♣ Qxx

OPENER	RESPONDER
1 ♠	1 NT
2 ♠	3 ♦
3 NT	Pass

Responder, with 9 points and a fine six-card suit, makes a game try over two spades. Opener, with a maximum and a fit for diamonds, gladly bids game.

When responder holds the 9- to 11-point hand with which he would have used the sequence

OPENER	RESPONDER
1 ♠	1 NT
2 ♣	2 NT

he can make the same bid over the two-spade rebid and convey the same message. However, he has the extra choice of raising opener's major to three:

OPENER	RESPONDER
1 ♥	1 NT
2 ♥	3 ♥

This would be his action with a doubleton in a side suit which promised ruffing value for a trump contract. Also, responder might try for the suit game if his hand is rich in aces or kings, but lacks the fillers that are so important for notrump play. A few examples:

OPENER	RESPONDER
1 ♠	1 NT
2 ♠	?

With ♠ J x   ♡ K 10 9 x   ◊ K J x x   ♣ Q x x, responder has an ideal 2 NT rebid.

With ♠ J x   ♡ K Q 10 x   ◊ K J x x x   ♣ x x, responder has ruffing value, and rebids three spades.

With ♠ J x   ♡ A x x x   ◊ A x x x   ♣ x x x, responder has no fillers, so rebids three spades.

With ♠ x   ♡ K 10 9 x   ◊ K J 10 x x   ♣ Q J x, responder is good enough for 2 NT in spite of the singleton spade.

RAISES

When the responder has three cards or more in opener's major, he knows that this will be the trump suit since there are at least eight trumps in the combined hands. His only problem is whether or not to go to game.

To resolve this problem, he has available two types of raise, one stronger than the other. The weaker and more often used raise goes simply

OPENER	RESPONDER
1 ♠	2 ♠

This single raise in a major is made only with a bad hand. The top limit is 9 points, counting distribution. (Add 5 points for a void, 3 points for a singleton, 1 point for a doubleton. Add 1 point for five trumps; subtract 1 point for three trumps.) Still, there is always a prospect of game, for a fit has been found.

The single raise shows a bad hand with trump support, and this description applies to a great variety of hands. With fewer than 5 points, responder would surely pass and with more than 9 points he would make a better bid, but there is a lot of room between these limits. The reason for all this room is that the major-suit raise is such a useful bid—making it difficult for the enemy to enter the auction on just those hands where you want to keep them out—*and a good system should let you bid it often.*

Opening bidder will try for game over the raise if he

has 17 points including distribution (for opener, add 2 points for a seven-card suit, 2 points for a void, 1 point for a six-card suit, and 1 point for a singleton), and will insist on game with 20 points.

Responder will accept an invitation to go to game if he holds 7 to 9 points, but will decline it with 5 or 6 points.

A few illustrative hands:

♠ K Q 10 x x	♠ J x x x
♡ x x	♡ 10 x x
◇ A Q x	◇ K J x x
♣ J x x	♣ Q x

OPENER	RESPONDER
1 ♠	2 ♠
Pass	

A minimum opening bid facing a pretty good raise. Two spades is the limit of the hand, and the bid will no doubt buy the contract although the opponents are probably cold for a lot of hearts or clubs.

♠ K Q 10 x x	♠ J x x x
♡ K x	♡ 10 x x
◇ A Q x	◇ K J x x
♣ J x x	♣ Q x

OPENER	RESPONDER
1 ♠	2 ♠
Pass	

Opening bidder here has substantially more than a minimum, but still not enough to make a try for game.

♠ A Q 10 x x	♠ J x x x
♡ A x	♡ 10 x x
◇ A Q x	◇ K J x x
♣ J x x	♣ Q x

OPENER	RESPONDER
1 ♠	2 ♠
2 NT	4 ♠

Opener now has the values for a game try. Since he has a flat hand with honors in all suits, he bids 2 NT. Responder has an 8-point raise, so he goes to game. With four trumps and a doubleton, he elects to play in the suit.

♠ A Q 10 x x x	♠ J x x x
♡ A x	♡ K x x
◊ A Q x	◊ x x x x
♣ J x	♣ x x

OPENER	RESPONDER
1 ♠	2 ♠
3 ♠	Pass

Opener has a fine suit with a weak doubleton on the side so he makes his try in spades. Here, responder has a 5-point raise, so he firmly rejects any suggestion that he go to game.

♠ A Q 10 x x	♠ J x x x
♡ A x	♡ K x x
◊ A Q x	◊ x x x x
♣ A x x	♣ x x

OPENER	RESPONDER
1 ♠	2 ♠
3 NT	4 ♠

With 20 points, opener does not *invite* game, he insists upon it.

Strong Single Raises

When responder has a fit for opener's major suit and a pretty fair hand (10 to 12 points including distribution), he has available the stronger raise. This takes advantage of the forcing 1 NT response, and goes

OPENER	RESPONDER
1 ♠ (♡)	1 NT
2 ♣ (◊ or ♡)	3 ♠

This sequence says, "Partner, I'm not quite strong enough to insist on game, but if you have anything to spare over your opening bid let's go on." Opener needs only 14 or 15 points to contract for game.

♠ K Q 10 x x	♠ J x x x
♡ x x	♡ A x x x
◊ A Q x	◊ x
♣ J x x	♣ Q 10 x x

OPENER	RESPONDER
1 ♠	1 NT
2 ♣	3 ♠
Pass	

Responder shows his 10 points in support of spades—he adds 3 points for the singleton—but opener, with his minimum 12, refuses to proceed.

♠ K Q 10 x x	♠ J x x x
♡ K x	♡ A x x x
◇ A Q x	◇ x
♣ J x x	♣ Q 10 x x

OPENER	RESPONDER
1 ♠	1 NT
2 ♣	3 ♠
4 ♠	Pass

Here opener has a little strength in reserve, and so cheerfully carries on to game.

If opener rebids his major over 1 NT instead of bidding a new suit, responder will raise him to three. This asks opener if he has any extra values.

♠ x x	♠ x x
♡ K Q 10 x x x	♡ A J x
◇ A x	◇ K Q x x
♣ A x x	♣ J x x x

OPENER	RESPONDER
1 ♡	1 NT
2 ♡	3 ♡
4 ♡	Pass

Responder is too strong to bid two hearts over one heart, so he bids 1 NT first. His bid of three hearts invites opener to go on unless he has a bare minimum. Opener, with a sound hand, carries on.

On rare occasions, responder may jump all the way to four over the rebid.

♠ x x	♠ x x
♡ K Q 10 x x x	♡ x x x
◇ A x	◇ K 10 x x
♣ Q x x	♣ A K x x

OPENER	RESPONDER
1 ♡	1 NT
2 ♡	4 ♡
Pass	

Had opener bid two clubs or two diamonds over 1 NT, responder would have bid only three hearts. However, the two-heart rebid is all that responder needed to hear—opener has a six-card suit, so responder wants to be in game even facing a minimum.

Note that the stepped major-suit raises—

$$1 \spadesuit—2 \spadesuit$$

with poor hands, and

$$1 \spadesuit—1 \text{ NT}$$
$$2 \diamondsuit—3 \spadesuit$$

with pretty good hands—conform to our general theory of bidding. The weaker hand calls for the higher initial bid, making it tough for the opponents to compete, while the better hand calls for the lower bid, allowing room for investigation of your own maximum contract.

STRONG RESPONSES

So far, we have considered responder's weak and moderately strong hands, with all of which he responds 1 NT or raises opener's major. With really solid values, which will probably make game facing even a minimum opening bid, responder can jump to 2 NT, jump to three in opener's major, or bid a new suit at the two-level.

Responder's jump to 2 NT describes a balanced hand of 12 to 14 points with stoppers in the unbid suits—a "weak notrump" opposite the opening bid. It rarely contains more than a doubleton in opener's major, for with three-card support the 2 NT response is to be avoided except with 4-3-3-3 hands.

This response is forcing on the opening bidder, and neither partner may pass until game is reached.

♠ K Q 10 x x	♠ x x
♡ x x	♡ A 10 9 x
◊ A Q x	◊ K J x
♣ J x x	♣ K Q x x

OPENER	RESPONDER
1 ♠	2 NT
3 NT	Pass

Responder, with 13 points, is too strong merely to *invite* game by responding 1 NT and rebidding 2 NT. He *forces* to game by jumping to 2 NT directly.

The jump raise (1 ♠—3 ♠, or 1 ♡—3 ♡) is, like the jump to 2 NT, forcing to game but limited. It announces at least four-card support, with 13 to 15 points, including distribution, in support of opener's suit.

♠ KQ10xx	♠ Axxx
♡ xx	♡ Kxxx
◇ AQx	◇ Kxxx
♣ Jxx	♣ x

OPENER	RESPONDER
1 ♠	3 ♠
4 ♠	Pass

Responder has 13 points in support of spades, counting 3 points for the singleton. Therefore he is too strong to *invite* game by responding 1 NT and rebidding three spades. He *forces* to game by jumping directly to three spades.

The most common strength-showing response is the take-out to the two-level in a new suit (1 ♠—2 ◇; 1 ♡—2 ♣; etc.) This is as strong a bid as either jump mentioned before; in fact, it may be much stronger since there is virtually no top limit. Responder announces that he too has the strength of an opening bid, and promises to bid again over opener's minimum rebid. Still, the takeout is not quite forcing to game, for although the partnership has the bulk of the high cards there may be a misfit. However, *when either opener or responder supports his partner's suit or bids notrump, the force to game applies.* Let us look at a few basic auctions:

♠ KQ10xx	♠ Axx
♡ xx	♡ KJx
◇ AQx	◇ xx
♣ Jxx	♣ KQxxx

OPENER	RESPONDER
1 ♠	2 ♣
2 ♠	3 ♠
4 ♠	Pass

With 13 points in high cards, responder wants to go to game. His hand is unsuitable for the jump to 2 NT (no diamond stopper) or the jump to three spades (only three spades) so he bids his best suit and then supports spades secondarily. This describes a very good hand with fair trump support.

Opener has a minimum, but doesn't even consider passing three spades, for responder has forced to game. Had responder been doubtful about game, he would have bid 1 NT, not two clubs, before raising spades.

♠ K Q 10 x x	♠ x
♡ x x	♡ A 10 9 x
◇ A Q x	◇ K J x
♣ J x x	♣ K Q x x x

OPENER	RESPONDER
1 ♠	2 ♣
2 ♠	2 NT
3 NT	Pass

Here, too, responder has 13 points and wants to go to game. With an unbalanced hand, he can't bid 2 NT directly so he bids two clubs and rebids 2 NT over two spades.

Opener has a dead minimum, but carries on to 3 NT since responder has forced to game. If more than a minimum opening were needed for game, responder would have bid 1 NT over one spade and would then have rebid 2 NT to ask opener if he had extra values.

♠ K Q 10 x x	♠ x
♡ x x	♡ A J 9 x x x
◇ A Q x	◇ x x
♣ J x x	♣ K Q x x

OPENER	RESPONDER
1 ♠	2 ♡
2 ♠	3 ♡
Pass	

Now responder has only 10 points in high cards, but his 6-4-2-1 distribution and fine six-card suit allow him to take out to two hearts anyway. However, he is careful to rebid three hearts over two spades and give opening bidder a chance to quit under game.

Opener has a minimum without a good fit, so he is glad to pass.

♠ K J x x x x x	♠ x
♡ x	♡ A J 10 x x x
◇ A Q x	◇ x
♣ x x	♣ K Q x x x

OPENER	RESPONDER
1 ♠	2 ♡
2 ♠	3 ♣
3 ♠	Pass

Both partners counted a lot for distribution in order to make their first bids. Therefore although each one likes his hand, neither can go to game until partner shows support. Distribution must be discounted in face of a misfit.

What are the minimum requirements for responder's new suit bid at the two-level? In general, he needs close to the strength for an opening bid. If he has no extraordinary distributional feature and intends to rebid 2 NT:

$$1 \spadesuit—2 \clubsuit$$
$$2 \spadesuit—2 \text{ NT}$$

he needs about 12 points in high cards. If he intends to support opener's suit on his next turn:

$$1 \heartsuit—2 \clubsuit$$
$$2 \diamondsuit—2 \heartsuit$$

he needs 13 points in support, counting distribution. These minimum values can never be shaded down, because these auctions force opener to keep on bidding until game is reached, even if he holds a bare minimum.

However, responder may take more liberties when he has a long strong suit, for he can rebid this suit and give opener a chance to pass under game. It is difficult to set a minimum requirement in points, for so much depends on the solidity of the suit. A hand like

♠ x   ♡ x x   ◇ A Q J x x x   ♣ x x x

has only 7 points in high cards, but it is worth a two-diamond response to one spade or one heart. After all, it may take seven tricks at notrump if opener has two small diamonds.

However, as a rule, at least 10 points in high cards would be expected, even with a long suit. With less, responder can bid 1 NT first and still be sure of a chance to show his suit.

The key question for responder to ask himself is, "Can my hand make a game facing a *minimum* opening bid with a fair fit for my suit?" If the answer is "yes," responder may bid his suit at the two-level; if it is "no," he must first respond 1 NT. However, no matter which way responder decides on close hands, he must never forget that *when he has responded at the two-level because of his length, not his strength, his second response must be a rebid of his suit.*

When responder has a two-suited hand, it becomes much more dangerous for him to take out to the two-level without solid, high card strength. Only by rebidding his first suit can responder sign off—when he bids a second suit, responder's hand is still unlimited, and opener must keep on bidding even with a minimum. Auctions like:

OPENER	RESPONDER		OPENER	RESPONDER
1 ♠	2 ♡		1 ♡	2 ◇
2 ♠	3 ♣		2 ♡	3 ♣

OPENER	RESPONDER
1 ♠	2 ♣
2 ◇	2 ♡

are reserved for responder's really strong hands, for they are forcing on opener. Usually, responder bids a second suit to avoid limiting his hand. For example, with

♠ xx   ♡ AJ9xxx   ◇ xx   ♣ AKx

responder will bid

OPENER	RESPONDER
1 ♠	2 ♡
2 ♠	3 ♣

He is too strong to rebid only three hearts, for he does not want opener to pass with a minimum. With

♠ xx   ♡ x   ◇ AKJxxx   ♣ AJxx

responder will bid

OPENER	RESPONDER
1 ♡	2 ◇
2 ♡	3 ♣

Again he is too powerful merely to rebid his suit.

Of course, these sequences are also used with genuine two-suiters, if they are strong enough. With

♠ x x ♡ x ♢ A Q 10 x x ♣ K Q J x x

responder bids

OPENER	RESPONDER
1 ♡	2 ♢
2 ♡	3 ♣

This is close to the minimum for the auction. Responder doesn't really know where he's going, but his overall strength should provide safety wherever he winds up. But with

♠ x x ♡ x ♢ A Q 10 x x ♣ K x x x x

responder bids

OPENER	RESPONDER
1 ♡	1 NT

Now he is too weak to bid both suits, so he responds 1 NT. Remember, opener will bid his better minor suit over 1 NT unless he has a six-card heart suit; and if opener does rebid two hearts, the hand may be a dangerous misfit.

Opening bidder will seldom have a rebidding problem after one of the strong responses. After 1 ♠—3 ♠ (or 1 ♡ —3 ♡) he will bid four in his suit with any hand of minimum to medium strength. Of course, with substantial extra values he can look for slam. (See the chapter on "Slam Bidding.")

When the response has been 2 NT, opener raises to 3 NT if his distribution is flat. With an unbalanced hand, he may rebid his major or show a new suit to find a fit for a trump contract.

These strong response sequences are simple and clear-cut, for there is little choice of contract—it is virtually certain that the partnership will play four of opener's major or 3 NT. However, when the strong response is a new suit at the two-level, many more contracts are reasonable possibilities. Now opener must take greater pains to describe his hand to responder.

After

OPENER	RESPONDER
1 ♡	2 ♣

the only rebid by opener that does not promise additional values is two hearts, the rebid of his suit. If opener rebids two diamonds, he shows that he does not have a minimum —he has either very good distribution or extra high-card strength. With

♠ xx ♡ A Q 10 xx ◇ A Q xxx ♣ x

opener bids

OPENER	RESPONDER
1 ♡	2 ♣
2 ◇	

He has no high-card surplus, but the distribution raises his hand out of the minimum class. With

♠ xxx ♡ AKJxx ◇ AKx ♣ Qx

opener bids

OPENER	RESPONDER
1 ♡	2 ♣
2 ◇	

A rebid of two hearts is acceptable, but two diamonds is better, for it shows a good hand and allows responder to bid notrump if he has spades stopped. With

♠ xx ♡ A Q 10 xx ◇ A J xx ♣ xx

opener bids

OPENER	RESPONDER
1 ♡	2 ♣
2 ♡	

With this bare minimum, opener's first duty is to try to limit his hand. This is more important than showing diamonds at this point.

An exception: When the opening bid is 1 ♠, a rebid of two hearts over a minor suit takeout does *not* promise extra values. It may be vital to bid hearts; the major suit is never suppressed. With

♠ A Q 10 x x ♡ A J x x ◊ x x ♣ x x

opener bids

OPENER	RESPONDER
1 ♠	2 ♣
2 ♡	

even though he has a minimum.

The opening bidder has two other moderately strong rebids available after 1 ♠—2 ♣. He can bid 2 NT or raise to three clubs. Note that under the rule: "Game must be reached after a two-level takeout if either partner supports the other or bids notrump," both these rebids force to game.

The rebid of 2 NT shows a hand split 5-3-3-2, with 15 to 17 points. Generally speaking, some mild fit with responder's suit—perhaps a doubleton honor—is included. Opener must have stoppers in both side suits.

The rebid of three clubs after 1 ♠—2 ♣ shows at least three clubs to a high honor or four to the jack, with 15 points or more in support of clubs, counting distribution. This is a strong rebid, and opener must not use it merely because he has a club fit. With

♠ A K J x x ♡ x x ◊ x x ♣ K 10 x x

opener bids

OPENER	RESPONDER
1 ♠	2 ♣
2 ♠	

He will get a chance to support clubs later, for responder may not pass the minimum rebid after bidding at the two-level.

Since his minimum rebid will never be passed, opener does not *have* to use a strong rebid whenever he has the values; but as a general rule he should. Bridge is a partnership game and it's almost always a good idea to give partner as much information as possible. He may be able to use it.

OPENER'S STRONG REBIDS

All the hands we have given the opening bidder so far have been poor, drab minimums. Let's see what happens when he holds lively cards.

When opener has a big hand and hears a strong response from partner, he is in the slam range. These auctions are treated in the chapter on slam bidding. But most of the time when opener has a meaty hand he will hear, alas, a 1 NT response or a single raise of his major suit. Over the raise, opener can simply jump to game in his suit, but over the 1 NT response he may be in doubt where or how high to play. To show his power, he can jump in a new suit, jump in his first suit, or raise notrump.

The raise to 2 NT shows a solid 18 to a thin 20 points and a balanced hand. For example:

♠ A Q 10 x x   ♡ A J x   ◊ K x   ♣ K Q x

With this hand, you don't want to bid two clubs over 1 NT, for you want to be in 3 NT facing many hands with which partner would pass two clubs. Responder will raise to 3 NT with 7 to 8 points in high cards, or with any good-looking suit. If he bids a new suit at the three-level, it is a *weak* suit which he fears will be useless at notrump.

♠ A Q 10 x x	♠ x
♡ A J x	♡ x x
◊ K x	◊ J x x x x x
♣ K Q x	♣ A x x x

OPENER	RESPONDER
1 ♠	1 NT
2 NT	3 ◊
Pass	

♠ A Q 10 x x	♠ x
♡ A J x	♡ x x
◊ K x	◊ A Q 10 x x x
♣ K Q x	♣ x x x x

OPENER	RESPONDER
1 ♠	1 NT
2 NT	3 NT

If responder supports opener's suit over 2 NT:

OPENER	RESPONDER
1 ♠	1 NT
2 NT	3 ♠

he has the "2½" spade bid, 10 to 12 points in support, and was too strong to raise directly. With any *poor* hand containing spade support, responder would have bid 1 ♠ — 2 ♠.

Only rarely will opener raise to 3 NT over 1 NT. This jump is not based on high-card values, for if a hand is too strong in points for a rebid of 2 NT, it is strong enough to open 2 NT originally. Therefore, this auction is always predicated on taking tricks—on a long, solid suit. For example:

♠ AKQ 10 x x   ♡ A x   ◊ K 10 x   ♣ Q x

is a fine 3 NT jump. A smattering of nothing in responder's hand will yield a play for nine tricks.

Opener will rebid his major suit over 1 NT with a six-card suit or longer. This may be the simple rebid already covered:

OPENER	RESPONDER
1 ♡	1 NT
2 ♡	

or the stronger jump rebid

OPENER	RESPONDER
1 ♡	1 NT
3 ♡	

This jump rebid is invitational, not forcing, and shows 18 to 19 points (adding to high-card count 2 points for a seven-card suit, 2 points for a void, 1 point for a six-card suit and 1 point for a singleton). If responder has a singleton in opener's suit, he will tend to pass unless he has 8 points in high cards, with which he can bid 3 NT. With a doubleton in opener's major, responder needs only 6 to 7 points to bid four of the suit.

♠ AKJxxx	♠ x
♡ Ax	♡ QJxx
◊ KQx	◊ Axxx
♣ xx	♣ 10xxx

OPENER	RESPONDER
1 ♠	1 NT
3 ♠	Pass

	♠ A K J x x x		♠ x x
	♡ A x		♡ Q J x
	◇ K Q x		◇ A x x x
	♣ x x		♣ 10 x x x

OPENER	RESPONDER
1 ♠	1 NT
3 ♠	4 ♠
Pass	

Opener's jump to four in his suit over 1 NT is a "gambling" bid, not a strength-showing bid. Responder, therefore, must pass. Opener may have, for example:

♠ A K J 10 x x   ♡ x   ◇ K J x x   ♣ x

Once in a while, if you're a good card-holder, you'll pick up a hand so strong that you want to be in game facing even the thinnest response. This mauler calls for a jump rebid in a new suit:

OPENER	RESPONDER
1 ♡	1 NT
3 ♣	

Frequently this will be a powerful two-suiter, like

♠ x   ♡ A K Q 10 x   ◇ K x   ♣ A Q J x x.

Or, it might be a hand rich in aces and kings, like

♠ A Q   ♡ A K 10 x x   ◇ x x   ♣ A K x x.

If you hold a hand with the pattern for a jump rebid, but too strong to risk a pass, such as

♠ A K J x x x x   ♡ A x   ◇ K Q x   ♣ x

you must manufacture a jump shift:

OPENER	RESPONDER
1 ♠	1 NT
3 ◇	

to make sure you get to game and to suggest slam possibilities as well. Note that the chance for slam facing a minimum response is common to all types of jump shift.

ONE HEART—ONE SPADE

Before leaving the subject of major-suit opening bids, one special case must be considered. Over an opening bid of one spade, responder must make a weak bid (1 NT or two spades) or a strong bid (any jump or new suit at the two-level). However, when the opening bid is one heart, responder can bid a new suit at the one-level. He will frequently make the ambiguous bid of one spade.

This one-spade response to a one-heart opening may be of almost any strength from very weak to very strong. Therefore, it is extremely important for the opening bidder to define *his* strength within narrow limits. For this purpose, he has three minimum rebids when the auction begins 1 ♡—1 ♠: 1 NT for a *balanced* minimum; two hearts or two spades with *unbalanced* minimums. With

     ♠ xx   ♡ KQ10xx   ◇ AQx   ♣ Jxx

opener rebids 1 NT. With

     ♠ x   ♡ KQ10xx   ◇ AQx   ♣ Jxxx

opener rebids two hearts. With

     ♠ Qxx   ♡ KQ10xx   ◇ x   ♣ AJxx

opener rebids two spades.

Note that opener may rebid a five-card suit over one spade, unlike over 1 NT. When opener bids a *new* suit over one spade, he shows additional value—at least 14 points.

The auction, as before, has begun 1 ♡—1 ♠. With

     ♠ x   ♡ KQ10xx   ◇ AQx   ♣ KJxx

opener rebids *two clubs*. He is strong enough to bid a new suit. With

     ♠ Ax   ♡ KQ10xx   ◇ Jxx   ♣ AQx

opener rebids *two clubs*. His hand is too strong for the balanced minimum rebid of 1 NT, which is limited to 12 to 14 points. He bids a three-card suit to show his extra values.

Opener's other strong rebids after the auction has begun 1 ♡—1 ♠ are: three hearts, four hearts, 2 NT, 3 NT, three clubs and three diamonds. All require exactly the same values as if responder had bid 1 NT instead of one spade.

One new strong rebid is added:

OPENER	RESPONDER
1 ♡	1 ♠
3 ♠	

This requires four spades, with at least 17 points in support (adding 1 point for a doubleton, 3 points for a singleton and 5 points for a void). For example:

♠ KQxx   ♡ KQ10xx   ◇ x   ♣ AJx

Responder has an easy time with his second bid as he knows a great deal about opener's hand by this point in the auction. He adds his points to opener's narrow range and he bids game, tries for game or signs off accordingly.

Almost all these sequences are logical and self-explanatory:

OPENER	RESPONDER
1 ♡	1 ♠
1 NT	2 NT

Responder has 11 or 12 points and is asking opener to bid game if he has close to 14 points.

OPENER	RESPONDER
1 ♡	1 ♠
1 NT	2 ♣

Responder has a mediocre hand and probably wants to play a partial in spades or clubs. Opener may pass, since this is not a forcing situation.

OPENER	RESPONDER
1 ♡	1 ♠
2 ◇	2 NT

Responder has 10 to 12 points and expects to go to game, unless opener has shaded his values for his strong rebid.

One type of auction could be ambiguous unless clarified —when responder's rebid is a preference in hearts:

OPENER	RESPONDER
1 ♡	1 ♠
1 NT	2 ♡

or

1 ♡	1 ♠
2 ◇	2 ♡

These auctions mean that responder was *too strong to raise hearts directly*. He must have a fairly good hand for the preference—at least 9 points in support of hearts. With

♠ A Q x x   ♡ Q x x   ◇ x x   ♣ Q 10 x x

responder bids

OPENER	RESPONDER
1 ♡	1 ♠
2 ♣	2 ♡

What then does responder do with

♠ A J x x   ♡ x x   ◇ x x   ♣ Q x x x x

if the auction goes:

OPENER	RESPONDER
1 ♡	1 ♠
2 ◇	?

The answer to this question is: *Don't bid one spade in the first place.* With a doubleton heart and a bad hand, suppress the spade suit and respond 1 NT. Now the preference back to hearts:

OPENER	RESPONDER
1 ♡	1 NT
2 ◇	2 ♡

warns of a poor hand.

When do you respond one spade to one heart with a bad hand? Well, you can do it when you have a singleton heart, and so are willing to pass two clubs or two diamonds. For instance:

♠ A J x x   ♡ x   ◇ J x x x   ♣ 10 x x x

Or, you can do it with a spade suit good enough to rebid over two clubs or two diamonds. For instance:

♠ A J 10 x x x   ♡ x x   ◇ x x x   ♣ Q x

However, beware of this last auction:

OPENER	RESPONDER
1 ♡	1 ♠
2 ◇	2 ♠

with really bad hands; partner has a strong hand for his two-diamond rebid and will likely bid again. A spade bust:

♠ KJ9xxx   ♡ xx   ◇ xxx   ♣ xx

can be described by one final sequence:

OPENER	RESPONDER
1 ♡	1 NT
2 ◇	2 ♠

This shrieks your weakness to partner.

This whole complex system of opening bid, response, opener's rebid, and responder's rebid, surrounding the major-suit opening bid must seem strange, and difficult in the reading. In practice, though, it works out to be very, very simple. The five-card major, the forcing, limiting 1 NT response, and the weak raise provide a sure and sound foundation for the bidding. This gives a feeling of ease and comfort to auctions that you have only to experience to appreciate.

VARIATIONS

Non-Forcing Jump Raise: When the bidding is opened with one of a major suit, and responder raises to three, he shows four or more trumps, with 10 or 11 points in support of the opening bid.

♠ Qxxx   ♡ Qxxx   ◇ x   ♣ Kxxx

Jump to three if partner opens with either one heart or one spade.

Opener may pass with a minimum opening bid since the jump raise is not forcing.

3 NT As a Forcing Raise: The response of 3 NT to an opening bid of one of a major suit is a forcing raise of that bid. Responder should have strong trump support of four or more cards, with 13 to 15 points in support. (This is exactly like the forcing jump raise described earlier in this chapter.)

If the opener has a minimum opening bid, he goes back to four of his major suit. If he has substantial extra strength he may try for a slam.

Short-Suit Tries for Game: After an opening bid of one in a major suit has been raised to two, opener may try for game by bidding his shortest suit (usually a singleton).

Responder jumps to game if his high cards are in useful suits; returns to a minimum of the agreed major suit if he has useless strength in the opener's short suit; or bids a short suit of his own if he wants to pass the buck back to the opening bidder.

♠ AKxxx	♠ Jxxx
♡ Axx	♡ Kxx
◇ x	◇ xxx
♣ KJxx	♣ Qxx

OPENER	RESPONDER
1 ♠	2 ♠
3 ◇	4 ♠
Pass	

After the raise to two spades, opener tries for game by bidding his singleton. Responder has a very meager hand, but all of his high cards are "working," and he should jump to game. If opener made a short-suit try in clubs or hearts, responder would sign off at three spades.

If responder held:

♠ Jxxx   ♡ x   ◇ Qxxx   ♣ Qxxx

he would bid three hearts after the short-suit try of three diamonds.

The short-suit try is used most typically after an opening bid of one in a major and a raise by responder to two. It may similarly be used in this sequence:

OPENER	RESPONDER
1 NT	2 ♡
3 ◇	

Opener has strong heart support and a doubleton in diamonds. He wants to be in three hearts or four hearts, depending on how responder likes the doubleton in diamonds.

Since the notrump is weak and the response may also be weak, the partnership may go down at three hearts. If so, the opponents must have half the deck (about 20 points in high cards, perhaps more) with a good fit in at least one suit. A minus score of 50 or 100 points is no tragedy.

Responder's bid in a new suit is not a short-suit try:

OPENER	RESPONDER
1 ♣	1 ♠
2 ♠	3 ♦

Responder's hand is almost unlimited; he may be trying for a slam rather than for a game. Opener should bid normally, assuming that his partner has a diamond suit of some kind.

Pre-emptive Rebids: When an opening bid of one in a major suit has been raised to two, opener may try for game by bidding 2 NT with a good balanced hand or three of a short suit if his hand is unbalanced. There is no need to use a rebid of three in the original major as a try for game, and this rebid may therefore be reserved for pre-emptive use.

OPENER	RESPONDER
1 ♡	2 ♡
3 ♡	

This should show a six-card suit in a near-minimum hand. Good opponents will not let you buy the hand at two hearts, so it costs nothing to take the push in advance.

In some competitive auctions the same kind of distinction can be drawn between competing bids and serious attempts to reach game:

SOUTH	WEST	NORTH	EAST
1 ♡	1 ♠	2 ♡	2 ♠
3 ♡			

South is just competing, not trying for game. If he wanted to suggest game, he could bid either 3 ♣ or 3 ♦.

Chapter 4

After the Weak Notrump

THE KEY to all auctions that start with the weak notrump opening bid is the fact that opener has, with his first bid, given a virtually complete description of his hand. Responder knows that opener's distribution is balanced, and knows within a queen what opener's strength is. Therefore the responsibility for determining the final contract is almost always responder's—he is the one who can add up the partnership's total assets.

The bidding sequences after a notrump opening are usually simple and clear-cut, for it is only rarely that responder will not know right away just where he wants the hand to be played. In fact, the most common pattern is for responder to name the final contract immediately. Look at this hand which was bid by many different partnerships and by us at a Masters Pairs tournament this year:

OPENER	RESPONDER
♠ A x x x	♠ J x
♡ Q x	♡ A J x x x
◇ K Q x x	◇ x x
♣ Q J x	♣ A x x x

Typical "standard bidding" expert auctions were:

OPENER	RESPONDER
1 ◇	1 ♡
1 ♠	2 ♣
2 NT	Pass

and

OPENER	RESPONDER
1 ◇	1 ♡
1 ♠	2 ♣
2 ♡	3 ♡
Pass	

and

OPENER	RESPONDER
1 ♠	2 ♡
2 NT	3 NT
Pass	

These sequences averaged five bids each and ended in contracts which went down from 1 trick (3 ♡) to 3 tricks (3 NT). Our auction went simply:

OPENER	RESPONDER
1 NT	2 ♡
Pass	

Now, although we, perhaps naturally, pick as an illustration a hand in which we arrived at a makeable contract while most standard bidders were being set, we are not proud of the accuracy of our auction but of its *simplicity.* This simplicity is important, for bridge is a game of concentration. The more you have to rack your brain in the bidding, the less mental energy you have left to devote to the play and to subsequent hands.

And the standard bidders had plenty of brain-racking to do on this hand. Should the opening bid be 1 ◇ or 1 ♠? On the most popular sequence—

OPENER	RESPONDER
1 ◇	1 ♡
1 ♠	2 ♣

should opener now bid 2 NT or give a preference in hearts? And if opener bids 2 ♡ here, should responder go on?

But we had no problems at all. The opening of 1 NT and the response of 2 ♡ were both automatic. Responder could not know that 2 ♡ was the perfect contract—for all he knew opener could have a four-card fit in clubs. But he did know two things for certain: 1) Opener's hand was balanced and so must provide at least some meager support for hearts. 2) Opener could have no more than 14 points, so there could be no game facing his bare 10 points. Thus responder could bid 2 ♡ over the weak notrump opening with absolute confidence that this was a reasonable, if not the optimum, contract.

After a weak notrump opening, responder's first job is to decide whether or not the partnership has the strength to go to game. This is not difficult—he simply asks himself the question, "If partner had not opened the bidding, would I have?" In other words, responder needs a hand strong enough for an opening bid to make game opposite a weak notrump.

If responder has a weak notrump opening himself—a

balanced 12 to 14 points—he can bid 3 NT over 1 NT. If he has a 1 ♠ or 1 ♡ opening, he can bid game in a major suit. With a 1 ♣ or 1 ◇ bid he can jump to game in a minor. Of course he is not obliged to leap right into the final game contract; he may wish to explore the possibilities of playing at 3 NT instead of in a suit contract or of finding a 4-4 fit in a major suit instead of playing at 3 NT. As you will see later in this chapter, many strong bids are available for this investigation. But responder may use these strong bids only when he has a hand of opening bid strength; when he is on the borderline of an opening bid, he is on the borderline of a game and may make a try; when he has nothing resembling an opening bid, he has nothing resembling a play for game and must pass 1 NT or sign off in a suit.

WEAK RESPONSES

The weak responses to a 1 NT opening bid are these suit bids at the two-level: 2 ◇, 2 ♡, 2 ♠ (2 ♣, as you will see later, is an artificial strong bid)—and jumps to three in the minors: 3 ♣ and 3 ◇.

Responder will sign off with 2 ♠ or 2 ♡ whenever he has a five-card or longer major suit and too few points for an opening bid. He should never try to guess that the hand will play better in notrump than in his suit—there is simply no way he can tell. But he does know that opener has at least some tolerance for his suit; 1 NT may be a very bad contract, but two in a major cannot be, for the partnership has at least 7 trumps. And there is another compelling reason to bid the major suit. The auctions 1 NT—2 ♠, and 1 NT—2 ♡ have effective pre-emptive value. They take valuable bidding room away from the opponents, who may be able to make a contract of their own when opener has a weak notrump and responder has a poor hand.

Suppose partner opens 1 NT, and you hold:

    ♠ xxx   ♡ QJxxx   ◇ x   ♣ Axxx

Bid 2 ♡. You have no opening bid so you want to sign off. You have a five-card major suit, so you bid it.

    ♠ Jxx   ♡ QJxxx   ◇ Qx   ♣ Axx

Bid 2 ♡. The same considerations apply even when your hand is semibalanced. Two hearts must be a reasonable contract.

 ♠ AKQxx ♡ xx ◇ xxx ♣ Jxx

Bid 2 ♠. Your suit is strong, but you would not consider opening the bidding, so you must not consider looking for game.

 ♠ AKQxx ♡ x ◇ xx ♣ Qxxxx

Bid 4 ♠, not 2 ♠. You have 11 points in high cards and 1 point for distribution, so you have an opening bid and should not sign off.

When responder has a five-card or longer minor suit and has less than the strength for an opening bid, he can sign off with 2 ◇, 3 ◇, or 3 ♣. Here, however, he has also the option of passing and playing in 1 NT.

Why may responder pass 1 NT when he has a five-card minor but not with a five-card major? It is because the useful pre-emptive bids of 3 ♣ and 3 ◇ increase the level of the auction by 2 tricks; responder must be quite certain that the hand will play better in a suit before he contracts for 9 tricks instead of 7. As a general rule, the jumps to 3 ♣ and 3 ◇ are made only with really unbalanced hands —those containing a six-card suit or a singleton.

This does not apply, of course, to the 2 ◇ signoff. Here the level of the contract is not increased so drastically; it is always reasonable to suppose that you can take one more trick in a suit contract than at notrump. So responder can bid 2 ◇ over 1 NT any time he has a five-card suit. But this bid has so little pre-emptive value (it actually invites the opponents to enter the auction in a major suit) that it should be used only when you want the enemy to bid— either because you have a very weak hand and want to escape a penalty, or because you hope to penalize them.

Suppose partner opens 1 NT and you hold:

 ♠ Axx ♡ x ◇ 109xx ♣ QJ10xx

Bid 3 ♣. You are too weak to make game, but should not pass 1 NT because of the singleton. 2 ♣ is an artificial strong response (see page 96) so you must bid 3 ♣.

 ♠ xx ♡ Kxx ◇ KJxxxx ♣ xx

Bid 3 ◇. Again, you are not strong enough for game. With a six-card suit you want to play in diamonds, and you want to make it difficult for the opponents to compete.

♠ xxx   ♡ Kxx   ◇ KJxxx   ♣ xx

Pass. You bid 3 ◇ only when your hand is unbalanced. You bid 2 ◇ only when you want the opponents to bid. The pass of 1 NT has more pre-emptive value than a 2 ◇ bid, for it may conceal a hand very dangerous to the enemy.

♠ xxx   ♡ xxx   ◇ KJxxx   ♣ xx

Bid 2 ◇. With this hopeless hand you must get out of 1 NT before the doubling begins. Your best chance is for *their side,* not your side, to play the hand.

This covers all the weak responses to 1 NT except for the most important one—the pass. On all balanced hands of 11 points or less, responder will pass 1 NT. Note that this sets a trap for the opponents, for responder may pass 1 NT with a moderately strong hand, knowing that no game can be made. The opponent in fourth position will then be risking a severe penalty if he bids. In this hand, for example:

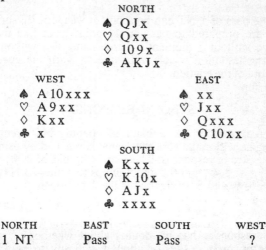

```
                        NORTH
                      ♠ QJx
                      ♡ Qxx
                      ◇ 109x
                      ♣ AKJx
     WEST                                EAST
   ♠ A10xxx                            ♠ xx
   ♡ A9xx                              ♡ Jxx
   ◇ Kxx                               ◇ Qxxx
   ♣ x                                 ♣ Q10xx
                        SOUTH
                      ♠ Kxx
                      ♡ K10x
                      ◇ AJx
                      ♣ xxxx
```

NORTH	EAST	SOUTH	WEST
1 NT	Pass	Pass	?

When North opens 1 NT and East and South pass, the West player has an insoluble problem. In this instance he will take a major set unless he passes. However, exchange the South and East hands:

```
                    NORTH
                 ♠ Q J x
                 ♡ Q x x
                 ◇ 10 9 x
                 ♣ A K J x

    WEST                         EAST
 ♠ A 10 x x x                ♠ K x x
 ♡ A 9 x x                   ♡ K 10 x
 ◇ K x x                     ◇ A J x
 ♣ x                         ♣ x x x x

                    SOUTH
                 ♠ x x
                 ♡ J x x
                 ◇ Q x x x
                 ♣ Q 10 x x
```

and the auction would be the same. North would open 1 NT and both East and South would pass. But now West can make four spades, and if he passes 1 NT he will collect only a filthy 100 points in exchange for his game contract.

The pass of 1 NT can be a potent weapon! Be sure that you are prepared to pass an 11-point hand like the one above without a moment's regret—and also without that telltale hesitation which will serve to warn the enemy to stay out of the auction.

STRONG RESPONSES

When responder has a hand of opening bid strength or more, he will make sure that game is reached by using one of the strong responses. These are: the bid of 2 ♣, jumps to 3 ♡ or 3 ♠, and the direct jumps to game—3 NT, 4 ♡, 4 ♠, 5 ♣ and 5 ◇ right over the 1 NT opening.

Direct Game Bid

If responder has no doubts about whether to play in notrump or in a suit, or about which suit to play in, he just leaps to the game he wants to play. Fully half our game contracts are arrived at this way, with no fuss and bother. If partner opens 1 NT and you hold:

♠ A K x x x x   ♡ x x   ◇ x   ♣ K Q x x

Bid 4 ♠. Any time you have a six-card major suit and an opening bid you can jump to game. Partner has at least two spades. However, if you had only a five-card suit you would want to investigate the desirability of a notrump contract.

♠ x x   ♡ A x x   ◇ A Q x x   ♣ K 10 x x

Bid 3 NT. You yourself would have opened 1 NT so you want to be in game. The 11-trick games in the minors seem remote, for partner has a balanced minimum; but 9 tricks at notrump are probably available. However, if one of your four-card suits were a major, you would try to find a suit fit before committing the hand to play at notrump.

♠ Q x   ♡ none   ◇ A J x x x x   ♣ A 10 x x

Bid 5 ◇. Only with a freak hand like this should you jump to a minor-suit game. Most often, when you hold a strong hand with a minor suit you will want to go slow and investigate the easier-to-make 9-trick notrump game.

Jump in Major

When responder has a five-card spade or heart suit, he may be doubtful whether to play in a major-suit game or in 3 NT. If opener has three cards or more in responder's suit, a trump contract is called for, but if opener has only a doubleton, notrump is probably best. Here is where the 3 ♠ and 3 ♡ responses are used.

The auction:

OPENER	RESPONDER
1 NT	3 ♠ (or 3 ♡)

has a very specific meaning. Opener is being asked "How many cards have you in my suit?" If he rebids 3 NT, he answers "Two." If he raises responder's suit, he answers "Three or four." These rebids are automatic—opener is not called upon to guess whether to play in notrump or in the suit; responder has taken the decision out of his hands.

```
    ♠ x x x              ♠ Q J x x x
    ♡ K x x              ♡ A x
    ◇ A Q x              ◇ K J x x
    ♣ K J x x            ♣ Q x

    OPENER               RESPONDER
    1 NT                 3 ♠
    4 ♠                  Pass
```

Here, opener has a flat hand, with no particular values for a spade contract and stoppers in all suits. But responder has not asked him to express his opinion; he has asked him "How many spades have you?" So opener bids 4 ♠ and is rewarded, for a heart lead will defeat 3 NT, while 4 ♠ is odds-on to make.

Stayman

All other strong sequences start with the response of 2 ♣ over opener's opening notrump. This is the *Stayman Convention,* an artificial, forcing bid which has nothing to do with clubs. Primarily, it is a method of finding 4-4 fits in major suits.

The 2 ♣ response asks opener, "Do you have a four-card major suit?" If opener has, he bids it. If he has both major suits, he bids 2 ♠.* If he has neither major suit he bids 2 ◇. No other rebids are possible.

When responder has a game-going hand that contains a four-card major suit, he can bid 2 ♣ to see if the opening 1 NT bidder also has four cards in the suit. In that case, the suit contract is likely to be preferable to notrump. For example:

```
    ♠ K x x x            ♠ A Q x x
    ♡ K x x              ♡ A x x
    ◇ J x x              ◇ x x
    ♣ A Q x              ♣ K 10 x x
```

* Opener will bid hearts later if it is obvious that responder was genuinely interested in finding a major-suit fit. For example:

```
    OPENER               RESPONDER
    1 NT                 2 ♣
    2 ♠                  3 NT
    4 ♥
```

OPENER	RESPONDER
1 NT	2 ♣
2 ♠	4 ♠
Pass	

Minor Suits

When responder has a long minor suit and is uncertain whether to play in his suit or in notrump, he first bids 2 ♣ and then bids his minor over opener's rebid.

OPENER	RESPONDER
1 NT	2 ♣
2 ◊ (2 ♡ or 2 ♠)	3 ♣ (or 3 ◊)

These are strong sequences and are forcing to game. In fact, these auctions frequently indicate some interest in slam, for if responder is willing to force to an 11-trick game, the right cards in opener's hand may produce 12 tricks. Here is a typical auction:

♠ A Q x	♠ x x
♡ Q J x x	♡ x
◊ A 10 x	◊ K J x x
♣ x x x	♣ A K J x x x

OPENER	RESPONDER
1 NT	2 ♣
2 ♡	3 ♣
3 NT	Pass

Responder is unwilling to commit the hand directly to play either in notrump or in clubs, so he temporizes and asks opener's opinion. Opener, with solid stoppers all around, elects to play 3 NT. Had opener's hand been, for example,

    ♠ xx   ♡ AKxx   ◊ Axx   ♣ Qxxx

he would have bid 4 ♣, not 3 NT. And had it been

    ♠ AKx   ♡ QJxx   ◊ xxx   ♣ Qxx

opener would bid 3 ♠ to show his stoppers (his 2 ♡ rebid denied a spade suit) which would enable responder to contract for 3 NT. All this may look a little complicated in print, but these are really common-sense auctions which you could figure out for yourself without ever reading about them.

Delayed Jump in Major

The last strong sequence to consider is responder's rebid of three in a major suit after first bidding 2 ♣. That is, one of these auctions:

OPENER	RESPONDER
1 NT	2 ♣
2 ◇	3 ♡

or

OPENER	RESPONDER
1 NT	2 ♣
2 ◇	3 ♠

or

OPENER	RESPONDER
1 NT	2 ♣
2 ♡	3 ♠

or

OPENER	RESPONDER
1 NT	2 ♣
2 ♠	3 ♡

These must be contrasted with the direct jump to three: 1 NT—3 ♠ or 1 NT—3 ♡. The direct jump, you recall, gives opener no option—he must play notrump with a doubleton in responder's suit, and must play in the suit if he has three or more. The delayed jump gives opener a real choice of contracts.

With the auction

OPENER	RESPONDER
1 NT	2 ♣
2 ◇	3 ♠

responder says, "I have a fine spade suit and am willing to play in four spades opposite a doubleton. However, if you have all your values in the side suits it might be better to play 3 NT even if you have three spades." Here are two such auctions:

♠ xxx	♠ KQJ10x
♡ KQx	♡ Axx
◇ Qxx	◇ Kxx
♣ AQxx	♣ xx

OPENER	RESPONDER
1 NT	2 ♣
2 ◊	3 ♠
3 NT	Pass

Opener has stoppers in all side suits and no particular values for playing in spades, so he bids 3 NT. But here:

♠ A x	♠ K Q J 10 x
♡ K x	♡ A x x
◊ Q 10 x x	◊ K x x
♣ K x x x x	♣ x x

OPENER	RESPONDER
1 NT	2 ♣
2 ◊	3 ♠
4 ♠	Pass

opener has ruffing value for a spade contract and so bids game in the suit despite his doubleton trump.

IN-BETWEEN HANDS

When opener bids 1 NT and responder is on the border-line of an opening bid, the partnership is on the border-line of a game. Now responder is too weak to force to game with one of the strong responses and too strong to sign off with one of the weak responses. He wants to give opener the choice of going to game or of staying at a partial contract.

First, what is a borderline hand? It is a hand that is one point light for an opening bid but that has some extra feature—a long suit, a four-card major—that might produce a game facing a fit. Or, it is a hand that meets the bare minimum requirements for an opening bid but that has some flaw—a weak, long suit, a concentration of high cards in the short suits—that makes game doubtful. Here are some examples:

1. ♠ A K J x x x   ♡ x   ◊ J 10 x x   ♣ x x
2. ♠ x x   ♡ K J x x   ◊ A 10 x x   ♣ K x x
3. ♠ Q J x   ♡ x x   ◊ K x x   ♣ A J 10 x x
4. ♠ Q x x x x   ♡ A K x   ◊ Q x x x   ♣ x
5. ♠ K Q x   ♡ J x x   ◊ K Q J   ♣ x x x x

Hands 1, 2, and 3 are just under opening bids, each counting to 11 points. But Hand 1 will produce a game if opener has good values for a spade contract. Hand 2 may make four hearts if opener has a four-card fit. Hand 3 might provide enough tricks to bring home 3 NT if opener has a maximum. So in all three cases, opener must be given a chance to go to game.

Hands 4 and 5, however, both count up to 12 points, enough to open. But Hand 4, with its skinny 11 points in high cards and its anemic suit, will make game only if opener has a spade fit. And Hand 5 has such a horrid 12 points that opener will need more than a minimum for 3 NT. So in these cases, opener must be given a chance to stay out of game.

1 NT—2 NT

The simplest of the "chance-giving" auctions is the raise to 2 NT. With this raise responder says to opener, "Bid 3 NT with 13 or 14 points; pass with 12."

Has it been disturbing you that, if you raise partner's weak NT opening to 3 NT when you have 12 points, you may be in a game with only 24 points in the combined hands? Don't worry! 24 points will make 3 NT more often than not *when they are split evenly between the two hands.*

Facing a 24-point hand you probably need 4 points, or 28 in all for game; facing an 18-point hand you want 8 points, or 26 total. This is because there is a lot of communication trouble between a very strong hand and a weak dummy—tricks are sure to be lost through inability to lead up to tenaces and lack of entries to cash long cards. But when the partnership hands are equal in strength, the maximum can be extracted. Twelve points opposite twelve will produce many more games than twenty points opposite six.

Still, 24 points in the combined hands is on the ragged edge. With a poor-looking 12 points it is better to bid 2 NT and make sure that the partnership has 25 points. Here are some of the bad features which should dampen responder's enthusiasm: 4-3-3-3 distribution; high cards in short suits; lack of 10's and 9's; isolated jacks. Raise opener's weak notrump to 2 NT, not to 3 NT, with:

♠ A Q x   ♡ J x x   ◇ Q J x   ♣ Q x x x
♠ K Q   ♡ J x x x   ◇ K Q x x   ♣ J x x
♠ A 5 2   ♡ 7 4 3   ◇ A 6 4 2   ♣ A 8 3

The raise to 2 NT is also made with 11-point hands containing a strong five-card minor. Here, responder expects his suit to win enough tricks to make up for his slight high-card shortage. But he is unwilling to be in game if opener has only 12 points, for then the partnership outweighs the opponents only 23 points to 17—not a preponderance of strength great enough for game. Raise to 2 NT with:

♠ Q x x   ♡ J x x   ◇ A K J x x   ♣ x x
♠ 10 x x   ♡ x x   ◇ A J x   ♣ K Q J x x

Major-Suit Sequences

Whenever responder wishes to suggest a 4 ♡ or 4 ♠ contract without forcing to game, he uses the Stayman 2 ♣ response to 1 NT. He bids 2 ♣ whether he has a four-card major suit and is looking for a 4-4 fit, or has a five-card or longer major suit and is looking for a three-card support.

With 11 points and a four-card spade suit, for example, responder should bid 2 ♣. If opener bids 2 ♠, responder then raises to 3 ♠. If opener rebids anything else, responder rebids 2 NT. An illustration:

♠ A K x x   ♠ Q x x x
♡ A x x   ♡ K x
◇ 10 9 x x   ◇ Q J x
♣ Q x   ♣ K x x x

OPENER	RESPONDER
1 NT	2 ♣
2 ♠	3 ♠
4 ♠	Pass

Opener could pass 3 ♠ on this sequence, but decides to bid game since he has a little extra for his weak NT and some ruffing value in spades. Now, change opener's hand slightly:

♠ A K x	♠ Q x x x
♡ A x x	♡ K x
◇ 10 9 x x	◇ Q J x
♣ Q x x	♣ K x x x

OPENER	RESPONDER
1 NT	2 ♣
2 ◇	2 NT
Pass	

Opener answers 2 ◇ to deny a four-card major holding, and responder bids 2 NT. This rebid announces that responder has a four-card major and specifically 11 points. Not less, for then he would pass 1 NT; not more, for then he would rebid 3 NT, not 2 NT. Opener would raise 2 NT to 3 NT on this sequence if he had 14 points. Here, with 13 points, he passes.

Responder also starts out with the 2 ♣ response when he has a long major suit of his own, but now he bids two in his suit, not 2 NT, over opener's reply.

♠ K J x	♠ Q x x x x
♡ x x x	♡ A K x
◇ A J x	◇ Q x x x
♣ K Q x x	♣ x

OPENER	RESPONDER
1 NT	2 ♣
2 ◇	2 ♠
4 ♠	Pass

Responder shows a long spade suit and an interest in game. Opener, with a fit for spades and a maximum no-trump bids game. Take the spade jack out of opener's hand, making it

    ♠ K x x   ♡ x x x   ◇ A J x   ♣ K Q x x

and he would bid only 3 ♠. (This responder might well pass, with his bare trump suit.) Take the little spade away from the opener, giving him

    ♠ K J   ♡ x x x x   ◇ A J x   ♣ K Q x x

and he would bid 2 NT, showing a maximum notrump but only two spades. Weaken this hand a little, to

    ♠ K J   ♡ x x x x   ◇ A x x   ♣ K Q x x

and opener would pass 2 ♠, for he has neither a spade fit nor a maximum NT.

There is one sequence in which responder is prevented from showing his suit. This is when he has a heart suit, and opener rebids 2 ♠ over responder's 2 ♣. If responder holds

♠ x   ♡ Qxxxx   ◊ AKx   ♣ Qxxx

he bids 2 ♣ over 1 NT, intending to bid 2 ♡ if opener answers 2 ◊. However, over a 2 ♠ reply, responder must bid 2 NT to limit his hand. He may not bid 3 ♡. As we have seen, 3 ♡ after 2 ♣ is a strong bid, forcing to game.

COMPETITIVE AUCTIONS

What is the effect on all these strong, weak and "in-between" sequences if the opponents enter the auction over the weak NT opening? The major change is that the 2 ♣ Stayman response is no longer available, so there are no more chance-giving auctions—responder must sign off or force to game. The general principle is that *any bid at the two-level is weak; any bid at the three-level is strong.*

In all the following examples, partner has opened with 1 NT, and your right-hand opponent has overcalled 2 ♡. What should you do with:

♠ KJxxx   ♡ xx   ◊ Kxxx   ♣ xx

Bid 2 ♠. You should show your suit even with a poor hand, when you can do so at the two-level.

♠ KJxxx   ♡ xx   ◊ AKJx   ♣ xx

Bid 3 ♠. With a game-going hand you must bid at the three-level (or jump to game). Opener will choose between 3 NT and 4 ♠.

♠ Kxx   ♡ xx   ◊ xx   ♣ KJxxxx

Pass. If your opponent had not intervened, you would have jumped to 3 ♣ pre-emptively. But with the opponents already in the auction, there is no pre-emptive value to minor-suit bids at the three-level. These become strong, forcing bids.

♠ AKx   ♡ xx   ◊ KQxxxx   ♣ xx

Bid 3 ◊. Now that you have a hand of opening bid strength you bid at the three-level. You hope opener can bid 3 NT (without the overcall you would have jumped to 3 NT yourself), and otherwise will play in diamonds.

♠ KQx ♡ Q10xx ◊ Axx ♣ xxx

Double. Your opponent has made a serious error. You and your partner have between you at least 23 of the 40 points in the deck, but the enemy are contracting to take eight tricks out of thirteen. And with a shaky trump suit! You should collect a big fat penalty on a hand with which you weren't going to bid a game.

Penalty Doubles

The opening of 1 NT puts responder in a particularly good position to make penalty doubles, for he knows just how much strength his side has and how much the enemy has. He doesn't have to fear that the opening bid was based on distributional values, and he knows that opener has at least two cards in the opponents' suit. What is more, an opponent who overcalls the weak NT is gambling on finding his partner with some cards. If responder has a strong hand, the opponent has lost his gamble,—there are, after all, only a limited number of high cards in the pack and with an opening bid, an overcall and responder's good hand out, dummy will come down with a Yarborough.

Therefore, the first requirement for a penalty double is high-card strength—enough to be sure that the hand "belongs" to your side not to the opponents. This means a rock bottom minimum of 9 points, and usually at least 10 or 11 points. Your holding in the trump suit can vary a great deal. With 11 points or more you might double with three trumps to an honor, or even, conceivably, three small. With 9 or 10 points, four good trumps should be a minimum. But *never* cheat on the high-card requirements. If an opponent overcalls partner's 1 NT opening with 2 ♡ and you hold:

♠ xx ♡ KJ10xx ◊ Qxxx ♣ xx

you must PASS, not double. Not that 2 ♡ might make—it won't. But, warned by your double, the enemy may escape to another suit; opener will double, counting on you for high card strength, and there you are in the soup. When

the hand belongs to the opponents, you should be delighted to get a small profit. Pigs wind up on the wrong
end of the cleaver.

Since you base your penalty double primarily on high
cards, you will find that once in a long while the doubled
contract will be made. If your opponent has a seven-card
suit and a couple of singletons, your high-card strength
may not take enough tricks. You take a calculated risk
when you double, just as you do when you bid a slam; occasionally good bidding will get you to a slam that goes
down, and a doubled contract is sometimes fulfilled against
a sound double. If you never go down in a slam you are
not bidding enough slams; if the opponents never make a
doubled contract against you they must be stealing your
eye-teeth on many hands that you fail to double. The willingness to have the opponents make about one out of six
doubled contracts is essential to winning tactics.

But if they make many more than that, you are doubling
too freely. Beware of doubles on *points* when the points
are mostly in queens and jacks. These cards are fine for
offense, but are sometimes worthless for defense against a
suit contract. Be reluctant to double when you have a long
side suit with which opener may have too good a fit. And
learn to distinguish between doubling a suit that is bid
voluntarily by an opponent and one he was forced to bid.

Suppose you hold:

♠ Axx   ♡ AJx   ◇ KQxx   ♣ 10xx

Your partner opens 1 NT and your right-hand opponent
overcalls 2 ♠. Here it might be well for you to forgo the
double and bid 3 NT. You have to defeat 2 ♠ a lot to
make up for the game you are sure you can make, and
your opponent probably has enough distribution for his
voluntary bid to prevent you from showing any real profit.
But if you have the same hand and the auction goes

PARTNER	OPPONENT	YOU	OPPONENT
1 NT	Double	Redouble	2 ♠
Pass	Pass	?	

you should certainly double. Your opponent has been
forced to bid spades and there is no reason to presume that
he has any great length. Now you may be able to set the
enemy four, five, or even six tricks and score substantially

more than the value of your game. In general, you can be more free with your penalty doubles of suits that an opponent has been compelled to bid.

One type of competitive situation has not yet been covered. What do you do when an opponent overcalls partner's 1 NT opening with, say, 2 ♠ and you hold a balanced 9 to 11 points, enough to make you sure that the hand belongs to your side, but not enough for game, and without the spade strength to double? A hand like:

♠ x x   ♡ K Q x x   ◇ K 10 x x   ♣ Q x x

You can't bid at the three-level and you want to act, so you clearly must bid 2 NT. Opener will not count on you for spade strength, for with spade strength you would double. Therefore opener will pass 2 NT only if he himself has the spade stoppers. Most of the time he will bid his best suit at the three-level, and you will pass.

You would bid 2 NT on this auction even if you held:

♠ x x   ♡ K Q x x x   ◇ K 10 x   ♣ Q x x

for you are not strong enough to force with 3 ♡. If your partner bids 3 ♣ or 3 ◇ over your 2 NT bid, you can then bid 3 ♡. If opener passes 2 NT you are probably in a reasonably good contract.

But be sure that it is really "your hand" before you use this 2 NT bid. It is very bad policy to do it with 7 or 8 points, hoping that opener has a maximum. If partner opens 1 NT, right-hand opponent bids 2 ♠ and you hold

♠ x x   ♡ K J x x   ◇ K x x x   ♣ x x x

you should pass, not bid 2 NT. Certainly you may be able to make 3 ◇ or 3 ♡, and the opponents may make their 2 ♠ contract. Still, if that is the worst disaster you ever have at a bridge table, you should be writing this book, not reading it.

The weak notrump is NOT designed to give you accuracy in bidding for partials; and striving for a precision which simply isn't there will get you only grief. By playing the weak notrump, you give up this accuracy in exchange for pre-emption. And remember, this pre-emption may have worked for you on this very hand. Partner may have four spades, and the opponents may go down in 2 ♠, when they could have made a partial elsewhere. Don't credit the enemy with omniscience—they know less about the hand than you do.

SCRAMBLING OUT OF THE ROUGH

We come, at length, to a most unpleasant subject—what to do with very poor hands when partner opens with a weak notrump. Nothing can get you a profit on these hands, but it is very important to minimize your loss.

The first rule is *if you haven't been doubled yet, get out of notrump.* The reason is that notrump contracts are the easiest to double for penalties. When partner's 1 NT opening is passed around to your opponent in fourth seat, he is going to double. (Simple arithmetic will tell you that if you have a very weak hand, he has a very strong one, for the cards must be somewhere.) And this double will be left in for penalties, for to penalize 1 NT all your opponents need is high cards, not strength in one particular suit. But if you bid a suit over 1 NT, what a difference! Now the opponent's double (1 NT—Pass—2 ♡—Double) is for takeout, not for penalties. You will be very unlucky indeed to find the trumps divided in such a way that the double will be left in. Almost invariably the enemy will bid a suit of their own and you will be out of the woods.

Of course, you may be dealt a hand which has no suit to run to—some mess like

♠ xxx   ♡ Jxx   ♢ xxxx   ♣ xxx

With this horror, bid 2 ♣ over partner's 1 NT! This will sound to partner like a strong hand, but the opponents' auction will soon enlighten him. And if they continue to stay out, you will pass opener's rebid—no matter whether it be 2 ♢, 2 ♡ or 2 ♠. Now everyone will know that your 2 ♣ bid was phony, but you will be in a suit, and suits are hard to double for penalties. Here is a typical hand:

```
              NORTH
            ♠ Kxx
            ♡ K 10xx
            ♢ AJx
            ♣ Qxx
  WEST                     EAST
♠ Ax                    ♠ QJ10xx
♡ A9xx                  ♡ Qx
♢ Kxx                   ♢ Q10x
♣ AJxx                  ♣ K10x
```

SOUTH

♠ x x x
♡ J x x
♢ x x x x
♣ x x x

NORTH	EAST	SOUTH	WEST
1 NT	Pass	2 ♣ !	Pass
2 ♡	Pass	Pass	Double
Pass	2 ♠	Pass	2 NT
Pass	3 NT	Pass	Pass
Pass			

Note that if South had passed 1 NT, West would have doubled. This would have been left in by East, and any subsequent run-out to a suit would then have been doubled also. But when South bid the Stayman 2 ♣, he created a situation where West's double of 2 ♡ announced not heart strength but over-all strength. Now to leave in the double East needed, specifically, heart strength and he didn't have it. Of course, East-West bid and made their game, but they lost the chance to inflict a disastrous penalty.

After a Double

The situation is different, and less hopeful, when partner opens 1 NT and your right-hand opponent doubles. Now if you hold a poor hand with no long suit it is more difficult to escape, since any suit you bid can be doubled for penalties, not for takeout.

Of course, if you have a five-card or longer suit, you bid it over the double. Suppose your partner has opened 1 NT, your right-hand opponent has doubled, and you hold:

♠ J 10 x x x   ♡ x x x   ♢ x x x   ♣ x x

Bid 2 ♠. Your hand has some value in spades but none in notrump. Also, 2 ♠ may not be doubled.

♠ x x   ♡ Q x x x   ♢ x x   ♣ K J x x x

Bid 2 ♣. This is not Stayman; it is a natural bid. Partner might conceivably make 1 NT doubled, but your side probably has less than half the high cards, so run for safety.

♠ Q J x x x   ♡ K x   ♢ 10 x x   ♣ K x x

Bid 2 ♠. No harm will come to you in 1 NT doubled, but it is better to bid 2 ♠ as you would without the double. This weak-sounding bid may trap the opponents into bidding at the three-level where you can probably hurt them.

♠ Kxx   ♡ AKxxx   ◇ Qx   ♣ xxx

Redouble. You have a game-going hand, so the opponents are already in serious trouble. You will either bid your game or penalize the enemy.

When you have no five-card suit you must decide whether or not to stay in 1 NT doubled. As a general rule, you should stay in 1 NT with 5 points or more. The opponents are unlikely to penalize you severely, especially since this sort of contract is much easier to play than to defend against. However, with less than 5 points, run for cover! You may or may not find a better spot, but you've already been doubled in 1 NT and your run-out hasn't been doubled yet. Perhaps your left-hand opponent—the doubler's partner—will be very short in the suit you run to and will have some long suit of his own to bid. You are already in deep trouble, and it is worthwhile risking a little deeper trouble for the chance of wriggling off the hook.

Suppose your partner opens 1 NT, your right-hand opponent doubles, and you hold:

♠ Q 10 xx   ♡ Qx   ◇ xxx   ♣ Qxxx

Pass. You are not overjoyed at the prospect of playing 1 NT doubled, but it may well be the best spot. The opponents have no great preponderance of strength, so partner may go down only one or may even make his contract. Also, the doubler's partner may not be strong enough to stand for the double, particularly if the doubler has a very strong hand.

♠ Q 10 xx   ♡ xx   ◇ xxx   ♣ xxxx

Bid 2 ♣. You may be jumping into the fire, but get out of the frying pan. Bid your lowest suit first in order to give the left-hand opponent maximum room to bid his suit. Your prime object, after all, is to get the opponents to bid. In addition, if 2 ♣ gets a vicious double, you can run to 2 ♠ without increasing the level.

If you are reasonably agile, there is no need to worry about penalties when the weak notrump is doubled. If you are set 300 or 500 points you will find that the opponents would otherwise have scored a game, so that you have lost nothing. And, although larger sets are a theoretical possibility when responder holds a complete bust, this has never happened to us in all the years we have played the weak notrump. It need never happen to you either, if you learn to get your neck off the block before the ax falls.

SUMMARY

You will have noticed that in all the auctions that start with the weak NT opening it is responder who controls. It is responder who decides that there is no game in the hand and picks the partial to play in; and it is responder who decides to bid a game and who almost always chooses which game to play. He determines whether or not to compete if the opponents contest the auction and whether or not to double for penalties. When the opponents double 1 NT, he is the one who runs when the partnership is in trouble and who redoubles when the enemy is.

Opener makes almost no decisions. When his partner forces to game, he goes to game. When his partner signs off, he passes. However, these auctions are possible:

	OPENER	RESPONDER
	1 NT	2 ♡
	3 ♡	
or		
	1 NT	2 ♠
	3 ♠	

Opener shows four-card support and a pretty good weak notrump. These raises are made as much for their preemptive effect as in the hope that this information will enable responder to bid game.

Opener may not decide to reopen the auction or double the opponents after his partner passes over an overcall. Nor should he run out of 1 NT doubled if responder stays there.

This is because opener has told his story with the opening bid. He knows nothing about responder's hand but responder knows almost everything about his. So opener must always accept responder's decisions as final.

VARIATION

Negative Doubles: Responder may double an overcall to show 9 to 11 points with only a doubleton in the over-call suit (instead of length and strength in the opponent's suit).

SOUTH	WEST	NORTH	EAST
1 NT	2 ♠	Double	

North may have some such hand as:

    ♠ x x   ♡ K Q x x   ◇ K 10 x x   ♣ Q x x

South will usually bid a suit, just as though North had bid 2 NT (as recommended earlier in the chapter). If South has a good four-card spade holding (such as Q-J-10-x) he is in position to pass the double for penalties.

When the partnership uses negative doubles in this situation, responder cannot double for penalties. Thus, in the example just given, assume that West's overcall is 2 ♡. North must pass, since a double would encourage South to bid spades (or some other suit).

If the overcall is passed around, the opener may reopen with a double, particularly if he has a doubleton in the bid suit and good support for the other suits. When this happens, responder gets his chance to pass the double for penalties.

When the opener has minimum values for his notrump, he may decide not to reopen on the theory that sleeping dogs don't bite. This tendency will cause the partnership to miss certain penalty doubles; but they will gain others (as when responder's negative double is passed by the opener).

Chapter 5

After One of a Minor

The opening bid of one in a minor suit *tends* to promise substantial values. The opener usually has a count of more than 14 points, either in high cards or in high cards plus distribution.

The opener cannot have a balanced hand of 14 points or less, for then he would have opened with 1 NT instead of one in his minor suit. Consider this very common beginning:

OPENER	RESPONDER
1 ◊	1 ♠
1 NT	

The opener must hold a balanced hand, for otherwise he would bid some suit or other at his second turn. Moreover, his high-card count must lie between 15 and 17 points. With less, he would pass or open with 1 NT; with more, he would find a stronger bid than 1 NT at his second turn.

The opener may have an *unbalanced* hand. If so, his hand is still likely to count more than 12 points in high cards. With less than 12 points, the opener may well decide to pass rather than open the bidding. (An aggressive player tends to open anything that resembles an opening bid if his suit is a major, but may pass the very same sort of hand if his suit is a minor.)

On occasion, it is true, a player may open a bare minimum unbalanced hand with one of a minor suit. (He *should* do so, for example, with 3 Quick Tricks even though his ace-king and ace count to only 11 points in high cards.) Then he should be on the lookout for a chance to indicate the disappointing truth about his hand. The standard way to do this is to make a minimum rebid in his suit:

OPENER	RESPONDER
1 ◊	1 ♠
2 ◊	

RESPONDING IN A MAJOR SUIT

Responder's first duty, if he has the values for any bid at all, is to show a major suit. A long major suit is, of course, desirable; but even a very weak four-card major suit is well worth showing.

Responder must remember that his partner may have a four-card major that he was unable to open—perhaps even *two* four-card majors. The minor suit named in the opening bid may be a three-carder. *Somebody* must make the first move in a major suit.

When the responder has only one major suit of four cards or more, he almost invariably responds in that suit. He may have a reasonably good holding in the unbid minor, but he tends to ignore that suit unless it is quite powerful (see page 116).

OPENER	RESPONDER
1 ◇	?

♠ xxxx   ♡ xxx   ◇ Qxx   ♣ Kxx

Bid 1 ♠. The hand is (barely) worth a response. Show your major suit, such as it is.

♠ KJxxx   ♡ Kx   ◇ xx   ♣ AJxx

Bid 1 ♠. The simple response is enough for the moment. You will show your full strength later.

♠ AJxx   ♡ Kx   ◇ xx   ♣ KJxxx

Bid 1 ♠. There will be time enough to show the clubs later, if need be. For the moment, your first duty is to show your major suit.

♠ Qxxx   ♡ KJx   ◇ Qx   ♣ AQxx

Bid 1 ♠. The game is probably in notrump, but there is no harm in looking first for a major-suit fit.

Similar principles are followed after an opening bid in the other minor suit:

OPENER	RESPONDER
1 ♣	?

♠ xxxx   ♡ xx   ◇ KQxx   ♣ xxx

Bid 1 ♠ (*Not* 1 ◊.) If the hand has any future, it is in spades; and an immediate response in spades is the most direct step in the right direction.

Several things are wrong with the response of one diamond. If partner bids one spade, you don't know whether to raise or pass. (If you then pass, you may miss a cold game; if you raise, partner may credit you with far greater strength.) If partner bids one heart, you will be reluctant to pass but even more reluctant to bid. If your diamond response is immediately overcalled by the next opponent with one heart, your partner may have to pass for lack of a hand good enough for a free rebid; and the opponents may steal, at 1 ♡ or 2 ♡, a hand in which your side can make two or three spades.

♠ xx   ♡ xxxx   ◊ AKxxx   ♣ Kx

Bid 1 ♡. If partner has a heart fit, your diamonds will be useful as a side suit. If partner has no fit for hearts, there will be time enough to bid the diamonds.

♠ xxxx   ♡ xxx   ◊ Ax   ♣ KQxx

Bid 1 ♠. Show the club support later, if need be. Your first duty is to show the major suit.

In general, as we have seen, the responder has no problem. He bids his major suit and awaits developments.

The responder has a choice of bids when he has more than one major suit of four cards or more. Then he must decide which major suit to bid. This choice is usually quite simple.

With major suits of unequal length, bid the longer suit first. Later, if it seems advisable, you may bid the other suit.

♠ xxxxx   ♡ KJxx   ◊ Ax   ♣ xx

Bid 1 ♠ in response to one of a minor. If spades are not supported, you will probably bid the hearts next.

♠ KJxx   ♡ xxxxx   ◊ Ax   ♣ xx

Bid 1 ♡ in response to one of a minor. If partner rebids in a minor suit or in notrump, you must abandon the spades. Partner has had the chance to show spades, and his failure to do so tells you that there is no spade fit.

With two 5-card major suits, bid the spades first. Show the hearts later.

♠ xxxxx ♡ AKJxx ◊ Ax ♣ x

Bid 1 ♠ in response to one of a minor. If spades are not supported, you will show the hearts next.

With four cards in each of the majors, you tend to bid the hearts. If partner raises hearts, well and good. If he rebids in spades, you will be able to raise. You thus have the chance to find a fit in *either* of the majors.

RESPONDING IN THE OTHER MINOR

We now come to the small group of hands with which your first response is in the unbid minor even though you have a four-card major.

This may be done when you can afford to make an immediate jump takeout (possible slam even if partner has a minimum opening bid); or when you have some reason to hope for game or slam in your minor if partner has only a weak doubleton in your suit.

For example, in response to partner's opening bid of one club:

♠ AQxx ♡ Kx ◊ AKQxxx ♣ x

Bid 2 ◊. Slam is possible opposite a minimum opening bid. The distinction between major and minor vanishes when you are considering a slam.

♠ AKxx ♡ xx ◊ KQJxxx ♣ x

Bid 1 ◊. The best game contract may be in diamonds, even if partner has a weak doubleton in that suit. There may even be a slam in diamonds if partner has a meaty opening bid, with two or more aces and some help for spades. (Whenever you must seriously consider game in a minor suit, slam cannot be too far out of your mind.)

♠ KQxx ♡ xx ◊ AQJxx ♣ xx

Bid 1 ◊. You are willing to bid spades at your next turn, even at the "reverse" level. If partner's first rebid is 1 ♠, you will raise to game, thus guaranteeing strong four-card support among other things.

♠ KQxx ♡ xx ◊ KQxxx ♣ xx

Bid 1 ♠. You are not interested in game at diamonds, and you are not able to reverse-bid the spades later. Follow the normal practice of bidding the major suit at once.

RAISING THE MAJOR SUIT RESPONSE

The opening bidder raises the major suit response if he has *four*-card support. Otherwise he finds some different bid to describe his strength and distribution.

It is not necessary for the opener to raise the major suit with A-K-x or some such strong *three*-card support and a hand of 15 or 16 points. With any such hand and balanced distribution, the opener can make a rebid of 1 NT. This shows 15-17 points and balanced distribution, and may well include strong three-card support for the responder's major suit.

Since the rebid of 1 NT shows strength, responder is likely to bid again; and then the support for responder's major can be shown. If responder must pass 1 NT, that is usually as good a spot as any to play the hand. (This is very different from the "standard" rebid of 1 NT, which shows a minimum opening bid: responder is likely to pass rather than bid, and the support for the major will never be shown.)

Since the three-card raise is unnecessary, the raise *guarantees* four-card support. We can go further: the opener *must* raise with four-card support for the major, and *cannot* raise without four-card support. (The opener may *reverse* or *jump* in a new suit before showing his four-card support, but he may not make a *nonforcing* bid in a new suit.) As a result, the partnership finds out at the earliest possible moment and without the slightest doubt whether or not a 4-4 fit exists in a major suit. (That is why the responder can afford to ignore a good minor suit in his zeal to respond in a major. He knows he will soon discover exactly what he wants to know.)

Given a hand with four-card support for responder's major, the opener need only know how high to raise. *Quantity* is the important consideration: the more points, the higher the raise. When the opener is on the borderline between one raise and the next higher raise, he may be swayed in either direction by the *quality* of his points.

The opener revalues his hand for support of his partner's suit. He counts high cards at their ordinary value, and adds 5 points for a void, 3 points for a singleton, 1 point for a doubleton. With this new count in mind, he raises according to the following schedule:

SUPPORTING POINTS	RAISE TO
15—17	2
18—19	3
20 or more	4 or jump in a new suit

OPENER	RESPONDER
1 ◇	1 ♠
?	

♠ A J x x   ♡ x x   ◇ A K x x x   ♣ x x

Bid 2 ♠. This hand is worth only 14 points and is therefore slightly substandard. You cannot afford to pass a hand with better than 3 Quick Tricks, but you must keep in mind the fact that partner expects your hand to be slightly better.

♠ A J x x   ♡ x   ◇ A K x x x   ♣ Q x x

Bid 2 ♠. This is maximum value for the simple raise.

♠ A J x x   ♡ x   ◇ A K x x x   ♣ K x x

Bid 3 ♠. With 18 points in support of spades, you have enough for a double raise. This is a minimum hand for so strong a bid.

♠ Q J x x   ♡ x   ◇ A K Q x x   ♣ Q J x

Bid 2 ♠. You have 18 points in support of spades, but the quality of those points is poor. You have counted too much for queens and jacks. Make the underbid rather than the overbid.

♠ A Q x x   ♡ K Q   ◇ A K J x x   ♣ x x

Bid 4 ♠. This shows strong 4-card trump support with 20 points or slightly more, counting high cards and distribution. (You are not likely to have *much* more than 20 points since you opened with only one diamond.) Your distribution is surely 4-4-3-2 or 5-4-2-2, since you would make a forcing bid in a new suit if you had a singleton or void suit.

♠ A Q x x   ♡ x   ◇ A K J x x   ♣ A x x

Bid 3 ♣. You will show your spade support at your next turn, completing the message. This shows a hand good enough to raise from one spade to four spades, but with a singleton (possibly a void) in the unbid suit. Note that it is necessary to make a *jump* rebid; a simple change of suit (*two* clubs instead of three clubs) would not show the strength of the hand and would not guarantee a singleton or void in the unbid suit.

♠ A Q x x   ♡ A x x   ◇ A K J x x   ♣ x

Bid 2 ♡. You will show the spade support at your next turn, completing the message. Note that a nonjump *reverse* is enough to show your strength, like the jump to three clubs in the previous case.* The reverse may be combined with a jump bid to show an even stronger hand:

♠ A J x x   ♡ A K x   ◇ A K J x x   ♣ x

Bid 3 ♡. You plan to show the spade support next. The jump reverse is used to show extra high-card strength in hearts, the suit of the reverse bid.

♠ A K x x   ♡ A J x   ◇ A K J x x   ♣ x

Bid 2 ♡. You plan to jump to four spades at your next turn. The jump will show exceptionally strong 4-card trump support. Comparison with the previous example shows that the jump is made in the suit that has unusually good top command, whether that is the side suit or the trump suit.

After a Major-Suit Raise

As we have seen, opener's raise of a major suit shows 15 to 17 points (not necessarily all in high cards). The auc-

OPENER	RESPONDER
1 ◇	1 ♠
2 ♠	

tion usually means that the opener has a hand of 15 to 17 points with a 4-card spade suit. A player who is accustomed to the strong notrump (16 to 18 points) may

---

* Reverses are often artificial (made in unplayable suits) and must therefore be treated as forcing. The only nonforcing reverses are those made after a response of 1 NT. The opener cannot then be concealing a raise, and his suit must therefore be honest—and nonforcing.

imagine that his partner has opened a strong notrump with a four-card spade suit.

Responder should have few problems from here on. If he has 15 points or more, he should try for a slam. If he has 10 to 14 points he should waste no time in getting to game. If he has 8 or 9 points, he should try for game. If he has only 5 to 7 points, he should pass quite happily.

There is no problem about passing or bidding game. Slam bidding is covered in another chapter. *Trying* for game is not always simple and is worthy of some study.

Responder may try for game by bidding three of his major, 2 NT, or three of some suit other than the major. The try of three of the major or 2 NT is clearly just a game try and may be passed; but a rebid of three in some other suit (even opener's original minor suit) is sometimes made when responder is considering a slam and is forcing for one round.

OPENER	RESPONDER
1 ◇	1 ♠
2 ♣	?

♠ A J x x   ♡ x x x   ◇ x x   ♣ K Q x x

Bid 4 ♠. With 10 to 14 points you go to game.

♠ Q x x x x   ♡ x   ◇ x x   ♣ A x x x x

Bid 4 ♠. Since opener has a 4-card spade suit, you may count your hand as though supporting *his* bid. In addition to the 6 points in high cards, you count 3 points for the singleton and 1 point for the doubleton.

♠ Q x x x x   ♡ x x   ◇ x x   ♣ A x x x

Bid 3 ♠. You count 6 points in high cards and 2 points for the doubletons. Try for game by bidding the major suit when you have five or more trumps or unbalanced distribution.

♠ Q x x x   ♡ K J x   ◇ x x   ♣ Q x x x

Bid 2 NT. Try for game with 8 or 9 points, and make the try in notrump with balanced distribution and most of your strength in the unbid suits.

Opener should have 15 to 17 points for his raise. He will go to game with 17 points, after a try; will stop below game with 15 points; and will use his judgment with 16 points.

OPENER'S REBID OF 1 NT

As we have seen, the opener's rebid of 1 NT shows a balanced hand of 15 to 17 points:

OPENER	RESPONDER
1 ◇	1 ♡
1 NT	

The opener would raise hearts if he had four-card support for that suit. He would show a new suit at the level of one if he could.

After the sequence 1 ◇ —1 ♡

♠ QJxx   ♡ xx   ◇ AKJx   ♣ KQx

Bid 1 ♠, not 1 NT. There is no need to suppress the major suit. Partner will play you for 15 points or more until you make the sign-off rebid of two diamonds.

After opener's rebid of 1 NT, responder can usually tell whether or not he wants to reach game. If the combined count is 26 points or more, responder can make a jump bid of some kind. If the combined count is close to 26 points, responder may make an invitational or exploratory bid. If the combined count is considerably lower than 26 points, responder should either pass 1 NT or work cautiously towards some safer part score contract.

After the auction:

OPENER	RESPONDER
1 ◇	1 ♡
1 NT	

♠ Kxx   ♡ QJxx   ◇ xx   ♣ AQxx

Bid 3 NT. Your own count in high cards is 12 points, and partner shows 15 to 17. The combined count is therefore 27 to 29. Since your distribution is balanced, you bid the game in notrump and relax.

♠ xx   ♡ KQJxx   ◇ xx   ♣ AQxx

Bid 3 ♡. Once again you have 12 points in high cards and know that the combined count of 27 to 29 points should be ample for game. The jump rebid asks for game, and the repetition of your suit suggests its length and strength.

♠ x x ♡ K J x x x ◊ x x ♣ A K J x

Bid 2 ♣. As usual, the change of suit suggests extra strength. (With most poor hands you would either pass 1 NT or rebid the hearts.) Since opener shows 15 to 17 points and you suggest extra strength, opener must not pass. This makes it unnecessary for you to jump to three clubs. You can make the simple bid and see whether opener can show a preference for hearts. (The jump to three clubs in this situation can be reserved for a powerful two-suiter, with at least 10 cards in the two suits.)

♠ x ♡ K J x x x x ◊ x x ♣ x x x x

Bid 2 ♡. Since you have only 4 points in high cards, the combined strength is only 19 to 21 points. Game is very unlikely. Even if there is no particular fit, however, two hearts should be a safer contract than 1 NT.

♠ x ♡ K Q x x ◊ A K x x ♣ x x x x

Bid 3 ◊. The jump shows the game-going strength; the raise shows the support for partner's suit; the failure to raise notrump suggests unbalanced distribution.

♠ x ♡ Q J x x ◊ K J x x ♣ x x x x

Bid 2 ◊. Game is unlikely, since the combined count is only 22 to 24 points and there is no major-suit fit. Your bid shows merely that you consider two diamonds a safer contract than 1 NT. If you were looking for game, you could have raised notrump, bid a new suit, or jumped to *three* diamonds.

♠ K x x ♡ Q J x x ◊ x x ♣ A x x x

Bid 2 NT. The combined count in high cards is 25 to 27 points. Partner will pass with 15 points, will go on to game with 17 points, and will use his judgment with the middling value of 16 points.

RESPONDER'S REBID OF 1 NT

Responder has the chance to bid 1 NT after the opener has made a rebid of one heart or one spade. A typical auction:

OPENER	RESPONDER
1 ♣	1 ♡
1 ♠	1 NT

Like most notrump bids, this shows strength within very definite limits. In this case, responder announces that he has *at most* 8 points in high cards. Since he has responded to the opening bid and has bid a second time, he must have at least 5 points in high cards.* Hence he has at least 5 points and at most 8 points.

Opener should know whether or not he wants to go on. If opener has the garden variety of hand, with 15 to 17 points, he need go no farther. Game should not be seriously considered. Opener should bid again only with unbalanced distribution or with a count of 18 points or more.

Responder should tend to bid 1 NT at his second turn whenever he has 8 points or less in high cards (unless he has exceptionally good distribution), since this will describe his strength very accurately.

Responder bids two of a suit (his own, partner's or a new suit) with 8 to 11 points. This indicates the sort of hand that will probably produce a game if opener has the usual 15 to 17 points; but the partnership may still hold back and stop below game.

Responder makes a jump bid of some kind (or bids the fourth suit) with 12 points or more. He knows that he wants the partnership to reach a game of some kind.

OPENER	RESPONDER
1 ♣	1 ♡
1 ♠	?

♠ xx   ♡ KJxx   ◊ Kxx   ♣ xxxx

Bid 1 NT. With 8 points or less, responder bids 1 NT at his second turn.

♠ xxx   ♡ KJxxx   ◊ Qxx   ♣ xx

---

* In general, responder needs 5 or 6 points to respond to an opening bid of one in a suit. He may shade this down a point or two if he has a singleton or void in partner's suit, particularly a minor suit. However, a response on only 3 or 4 points is a rescue rather than a true response; and responder will pass at his next turn unless opener makes a jump rebid or a reverse bid. In the example, opener's rebid of one spade is forcing if responder has a normal response; but responder may pass if he responded only to get out of trouble. When responder bids a second time, it is clear that he had a normal response (at least 5 or 6 points) at his first turn.

Bid 1 NT. The heart suit is rebiddable, but the *hand* is not. Show the weakness of the hand as soon as possible.

♠ Axx　♡ KQxxx　◇ xx　♣ xxx

Bid 2 ♠. You prefer four trumps for this raise, but you must make do with A-x-x, K-x-x, or Q-x-x if the hand as a whole is good enough. This is particularly true if you are short in the unbid suit, in which case *your* trumps will serve as stoppers.

♠ Jxxx　♡ KQxx　◇ xx　♣ Axx

Bid 2 ♠. The normal raise, with four trumps.

♠ xx　♡ KQJxx　◇ xxx　♣ Axx

Bid 2 ♡. The rebid at the level of two shows 8 to 11 points; the rebid of your own suit shows the strength of the suit.

♠ xx　♡ KJxxx　◇ Qxx　♣ Axx

Bid 2 ♣. This shows 8 to 11 points and coaxes partner to make a try for game if he has 15 points or more. If he has 3-card heart support, he will show it at this time; and if he has less in hearts, you are not eager to get to a heart contract.

♠ xx　♡ KJxxx　◇ QJxx　♣ Ax

Bid 2 ◇. If partner has 3-card heart support, he will show it at this time; and you will go to game in hearts. If partner bids 2 NT, you will raise to 3 NT. If partner bids three clubs, you will bid 3 NT in the hope of running six club tricks as the backbone of that contract; but you would tend to pass if your ace were in spades rather than in clubs.

♠ QJxx　♡ KQxx　◇ Axx　♣ xx

Bid 3 ♠. With 12 points or more, you make a jump rebid.

♠ Kx　♡ KQxx　◇ xxx　♣ AJxx

Bid 3 ♣. The failure to bid diamonds or notrump is significant, but the strength must be shown.

Let us return to the auction:

OPENER	RESPONDER
1 ♣	1 ♡
1 ♠	1 NT
?	

♠ KQxx   ♡ xx   ◇ Axx   ♣ AQxx

Pass. The combined count is 23 points at most. You have no reason to disturb the contract of 1 NT.

♠ KQxx   ♡ xx   ◇ Ax   ♣ KQJxx

Bid 2 ♣. This is not a strength-showing bid, but merely suggests that two clubs is a safer spot than 1 NT.

♠ KQxx   ♡ Axx   ◇ x   ♣ AQxxx

Bid 2 ♡. Game is not out of the question despite partner's announced weakness. Your bidding shows strong 3-card heart support and pronounced shortness in the unbid suit (diamonds). Partner should be safe at two hearts with almost any hand, and may be able to bid a game if he has the right hand for it.

♠ KQxx   ♡ AKx   ◇ x   ♣ AQxxx

Bid 3 ♡. This must be a strong hand, since you have jumped. It cannot show 4-card trump support, since with four trumps you would immediately raise hearts or make a forcing rebid. Hence you must have a fine hand with exceptionally strong 3-card trump support and marked shortness in the unbid suit.

♠ KQxx   ♡ Ax   ◇ Kxx   ♣ AQxx

Bid 2 NT. The raise shows 18 or 19 points, inviting partner to go on to game with only 7 or 8 points. He should be safe at 2 NT even if he has only 5 or 6 points.

♠ KQxx   ♡ Ax   ◇ x   ♣ AKQxxx

Bid 3 ♣. Partner is expected to bid 3 NT if he can stop the unbid suit (diamonds, in this case). Lacking a stopper, he may rebid a 5-card heart suit, show 3-card support for spades (doubtful, since he did not do so at his previous turn), or raise to four clubs. If he does the last, you will probably go on to game in clubs, hoping to lose only one spade and one diamond.

JUMPS TO 2 NT AND 3 NT

As we have seen, the opener's rebid of 1 NT shows 15 to 17 points. He may jump to 2 NT with 19 or 20 points, or with an exceptionally good 18 points.

OPENER	RESPONDER
1 ◇	1 ♡
2 NT	

♠ K J x ♡ A x ◇ A J x x x ♣ A Q x. The typical 19-point hand.

♠ K J x ♡ K x ◇ A Q J x x ♣ K J x. The exceptionally good 18-point hand.

The double jump to 3 NT does not show 21 or 22 points. The 21-point hand with all suits stopped should be opened with 2 NT to begin with. If the hand is weak in one suit, which responder has bid, the strength can be shown by a jump in a new suit.

The double jump to 3 NT is reserved for a hand with a solid or near-solid minor suit and considerable strength:

♠ K x ♡ x x ◇ A K Q J x x ♣ A x x

The hand, which counts to only 17 points in high cards, will produce 7 sure tricks, or 8 tricks if spades are led. There will probably be a valid play for game even if responder has a ghastly hand. (Moreover, the long diamonds may enable you to make the game even if there is no valid play for it. Opponents often slip when forced to make several discards.)

OPENER	RESPONDER
1 ◇	1 ♡
1 ♠	?

Responder jumps to 2 NT with 12 to 14 points. (Or with an exceptionally good 11 points.) He must also have balanced distribution and at least one stopper in the unbid suit.

Responder may jump to 3 NT with 15 to 17 points. However, when the responder has 15 points or more, the partnership is in the slam zone. Opener probably has 15 points or more, so that the combined count is likely to be at least 30 points. A fit, or the presence of another point or two may produce the slam. Therefore, responder should generally prefer to force by bidding the fourth suit or by making a jump rebid in his first suit.

Responder's New Suit

Any change of suit by responder is forcing for one round.

Responder may take advantage of the forcing nature of a change of suit in certain embarrassing bidding situations. For example:

OPENER	
1 ◇	1 ♡
1 ♠	?

♠ xxx   ♡ KJxx   ◇ xxx   ♣ AQx

Bid 2 ♣. You cannot bid 1 NT, since that would show a maximum of 8 points in high cards. You cannot jump to 2 NT, since that would promise 12 to 14 points. Nor can you rebid hearts or raise either of opener's suits. You must "manufacture" a response. If opener then goes to 2 NT, you will raise to game. If he does anything else, you will be in position to bid notrump yourself.

IMMEDIATE NOTRUMP RESPONSES

The immediate response of 1 NT to one of a minor suit denies a 4-card or longer major suit. It also denies the ability to raise the minor suit (see p. 128).

Ideally, the response of 1 NT should show 8 to 10 points. This is true when the opening bid is one club. If responder has a 6-point or 7-point hand that is not worth a club raise of some kind, he can manufacture a response of one diamond.

The response of 1 NT to one diamond is not quite so convenient. It is unwise to manufacture a response in a major suit. You may be obliged to bid 1 NT on any poor hand that is worth a weak response but not worth a response of two clubs. Hence the response of 1 NT to one diamond promises only that the hand is worth some kind of response, and denies ability to show a major suit or to raise diamonds.

The immediate jump to 2 NT over either one club or one diamond denies a major suit, guarantees a stopper in each of the unbid suits, and promises 12 to 14 points.

The immediate jump to 3 NT in standard American systems is used to show 16 or 17 points. We have never admired this use of the bid, although conceding that it is only occasionally fatal. We prefer to use the jump to 3 NT to show a hand that will produce a reasonable play for 3 NT opposite a psyche. If opener has a legitimate opening bid, he must go on; there will surely be a slam.

IMMEDIATE RAISE OF OPENER'S SUIT

In our system, the raise of one club to two clubs or of one diamond to two diamonds is *forcing*. The raise to three, however, is weak.

This is the opposite of the standard practice. We were led to this practice by logic rather than contrariness. The logic is similar to the situation in the major suits where a raise to three quite generally shows a stronger hand than a raise to four.

It should be a fundamental principle of any well-regulated bidding system that you keep the bidding low when you are strong enough to welcome an opponent's bid, and that you jack the bidding up as high as you safely can when you are too weak to handle competitive bidding.

The strong single raise of a minor suit keeps the bidding low when the partnership is strong. The weak double raise of a minor suit gets the partnership to a reasonably safe high contract when the partnership is weak.

Simple and logical. All that remains is to list the requirements and to show how the bidding develops.

Begin with the double raise. It must be based on 5 or more trumps, since the opener often has only a 3-card suit. It must deny a major suit, for obvious reasons. It must warn the opener that there is no game if he has the usual 15- to 17-point hand. Hence responder must have a maximum of 8 points in high cards; and he should not have such freakish distribution as to yield a reasonable play for game in the minor suit.

For example, after partner's opening bid of one club:

♠ xxx   ♡ xx   ◊ Kxx   ♣ Qxxxx

Bid 3 ♣. A typical hand of average value for this preemptive bid. If partner cannot make three clubs, the opponents should be able to make at least a part score. Like most shutout bids, it may spur the opponents into bidding, in which case they may come a cropper because of the lack of maneuvering space.

♠ xxx   ♡ xx   ◊ xx   ♣ Jxxxxx

Bid 3 ♣ if not vulnerable against vulnerable opponents. The opponents probably have a game, but you may steal the hand for a small loss. The jump is too dangerous if you are vulnerable, but you might jump to three of partner's suit without as much as a jack if you had a six-card suit and a singleton.

The single raise begins where the double raise leaves off. The minimum value is about 9 points in high cards, enough to yield a play for game if partner has towards the upper end of the expected 15 to 17 points. The maximum value is some 20-odd points, enough for an immediate jump in a new suit.

The forcing single raise in a minor suit denies a four-card major suit. As always, the first duty of the responder is to show a major if he can.

In general, the raise shows four or more trumps. By way of exception, the raise of one diamond to two diamonds may be based on strong 3-card support (with length in clubs, since major-suit length is out of the question).

For example, in response to one club:

♠ xxx   ♡ Kxx   ◊ Ax   ♣ Qxxxx

Bid 2 ♣. Just the minimum of 9 points, but game is likely if partner has 16 points or more.

♠ xxx   ♡ Kx   ◊ Axxx   ♣ Qxxx

Bid 1 ◊. The raise should show greater values, either in distribution or high cards.

♠ xx   ♡ Kx   ◊ AQxx   ♣ KJxxx

Bid 2 ♣. Raise the clubs first; there will be a firm foundation for any further bidding. You expect to show the diamonds later.

AFTER THE RAISE

The opener has a very simple future after a double raise in his minor suit. Nine times out of ten opener must pass.

Responder has a poor hand, and opener can seldom hope to make game opposite such slight values. If vulnerable, the opener may count on his partner for about 5 or 6 points in high cards or, at least, very good distribution. If not vulnerable, the opener knows only that his partner has five or more trumps, a fear of the opponents, and a fair amount of impudence.

Opener may bid 3 NT if he is just barely short of an opening bid of 2 NT. He may bid game in his minor suit if he has an exceptionally powerful hand and good distribution. If doubled at game, however, he should refrain from redoubling. Partner may show up with more impudence than values.

Life is more complex after a single raise.

To begin with the raise is forcing for one round. Responder will clarify the nature of his hand at his next turn, but first it is up to the opener to describe his own hand.

If the opener has a weak unbalanced hand, he simply goes on to three of his suit. Responder will pass this if he has only 9 points or so. If responder goes on, he has been warned. He should read the opener for about 3 Quick Tricks, a suit of at least 5 cards, and either a singleton or two doubletons (usually a singleton or void).

If the opener has only three cards in the minor suit he has bid, he rebids in notrump. Responder has no major suit, and opener has only a moderate fit for the minor suit that has been bid and raised. The future of the hand is almost undoubtedly in notrump. Opener bids 2 NT with 15 to 17 points, but jumps to 3 NT with 18 or 19 points.

Responder should have no trouble in determining his best course. He counts points to see if 3 NT is the limit of the partnership values. Over 2 NT, he sometimes will go on to three of the minor to show minimum values with an unbalanced hand.

If the opener has four or more cards in the minor suit that has been bid and raised, he may rebid in a new suit. Such a bid may be based on a suit of four or more cards, but does not guarantee it; the bid promises a stopper and asks partner to cooperate in the search for the best game contract.

The search may be short and simple or long and devious, depending on the nature of the partnership hands.

♠ A x x	♠ K x x
♡ K Q x	♡ x x
◊ A Q x x x	◊ K J x x
♣ x x	♣ A J x x

OPENER	RESPONDER
1 ◇	2 ◇
2 ♠ (1)	3 ♣ (2)
3 NT (3)	

(1) A stopper in spades. The diamonds are a true suit. Opener might bid two hearts rather than two spades but prefers to discourage a spade opening lead, if possible.

(2) A stopper in clubs. Hearts must be unstopped, since responder would be happy to bid notrump if he had stoppers in *both* of the unbid suits.

(3) The unbid suit is no threat.

How would this hand be bid by "standard" methods? The opening bid would be one diamond, and the response would be a jump to three diamonds. Opener might bid three notrump, taking the risk that clubs are wide open. If opener, instead, bids three spades, responder must now guess about the hearts. If the opener's second bid is three hearts, the responder can safely bid three notrump, but the partnership is on sure ground only when the opener happens to pick the right suit to rebid. Even this safety is impossible if the opener's only side strength is in clubs: if he bids four clubs, he has gone past 3 NT; if, instead, he bids 3 NT, he must rely on his partner to stop *both* of the unbid suits.

This does not mean that standard bidding will always lead you astray. It means only that guesswork has taken the place of logic.

Change two of the suits in the opener's hand, and see how the bidding goes:

♠ A x x	♠ K x x
♡ x x	♡ x x
◇ A Q x x x	◇ K J x x
♣ K Q x	♣ A J x x

OPENER	RESPONDER
1 ◇	2 ◇
2 ♠ (1)	3 ♣ (2)
3 ◇ (3)	3 ♠ (4)
4 ◇ (5)	5 ◇ (6)

(1) As before, a stopper in spades. The diamonds are a real suit.

(2) A stopper in clubs, none in hearts.

(3) Cannot bid 3 NT for lack of a stopper in the unbid

suit. It should now be obvious to both partners (and to the opponents also, if they are listening carefully) that the hearts are wide open.

(4) Good 3-card support for spades. If the opener has a real spade suit, this may lead to a sound game contract in the major.

(5) Sorry, partner, the spades are not playable. The hand is close to the minimum value of 15 points, since a 17-point hand would jump to five diamonds at this stage.

(6) A slight stretch. A conservative player might pass; an aggressive player goes to game.

All avenues to game have been explored, and the end product is a fine, logical contract. Five diamonds is virtually unbeatable; 3 NT is doomed by the highly probable heart opening lead.

How would this hand be bid by standard methods? As before, the opening bid is one diamond, raised by responder to three diamonds. Now opener may land in the soup in one short move by a bid of three notrump. If, instead, opener bids three spades, responder has an unsolvable problem. If he bids three notrump, the hearts may be wide open; and if he bids anything else, he may miss the only makeable game (by going past 3 NT).

There is no magic in this distinction between scientific bidding and standard bidding. The difference lies only in the fact that you have more room to explore when you keep the bidding low.

THE RESPONSE OF TWO CLUBS

There is something special about a response of two clubs when your partner opens with one diamond.

As we have seen, when the opening bid is one spade or one heart, a response of two clubs shows a readiness to play game opposite even a minimum opening bid.

It isn't necessary to be so rigid when the opening bid is one diamond. It is seldom necessary for responder to bid two clubs with a *good* hand: he can bid one of a major, or raise to two diamonds, or jump in notrump. When he does bid two clubs as the first move with a good hand, he will have an unmistakably strong rebid in mind: a bid in a new suit, a jump in notrump, a healthy diamond raise, or the like.

It is, however, necessary for the responder to bid two

clubs when he has strong clubs but a weak hand. He is also allowed to bid two clubs with a *mediocre* hand—a completely solid club suit, or a nearly solid suit with a side ace or king.

♠ xx   ♡ xxx   ◇ xx   ♣ AKQJxx

Bid 2 ♣ in response to 1 ◇. If partner bids 2 NT, you will gladly go on to 3 NT. If partner bids two diamonds or two of a major, you will bid three clubs.

♠ Kx   ♡ xxx   ◇ xx   ♣ KQJxxx

Bid 2 ♣ in response to 1 ◇. If partner bids 2 NT, you will go on to 3 NT. If, instead, partner bids two hearts, you will bid 2 NT. If partner's rebid is two spades, you will bid three clubs.

♠ xx   ♡ xxx   ◇ xx   ♣ KQJxxx

Bid 2 ♣ in response to 1 ◇. Pass if partner rebids 2 ◇; bid 3 ♣ over 2 NT or two of a major.

As may be seen, the idea is to try for 3 NT, with the long club suit as the chief source of tricks. The opener should rebid 2 NT if he has both majors stopped. He should bid his stopper if he has only one of the majors stopped. If responder's second bid is three clubs, opener must not go on unless he himself holds a high club honor and stoppers in both major suits.

OPENER'S REBID OF TWO CLUBS

There is something special about this auction:

OPENER	RESPONDER
1 ◇	1 ♠ or 1 ♡
2 ♣	

The opener may have simply a two-suiter with at least five cards in each of the minor suits. If so, he should be willing to bid up to three clubs or three diamonds.

There is another possibility. The opener may have strength of a different kind. He is willing to bid up to 2 NT or three of a suit.

The responder is strongly urged (virtually forced) to make a second response, even if he has barely the values for his first response. Responder tends to rebid a major suit of five or more cards. With a poor hand and only a 4-card major suit, responder may mark time with a preference bid of two diamonds. With a 4-card major and more than 6 or 7 points, responder may bid a new suit, bid 2 NT or raise to three clubs.

Responder need not commit himself immediately, for the opener has promised to bid again. Opener will bid three clubs if he has the routine two-suiter; will show support for responder's major with good three-card support and about 18 supporting points; or will bid 2 NT with about 18 points in high cards.

After the auction:

OPENER	RESPONDER
1 ◇	1 ♠
?	

♠ xx   ♡ x   ◇ AQJxx   ♣ KQxxx

Bid 2 ♣. You expect to bid three clubs next, thus showing a routine two-suiter.

♠ xxx   ♡ x   ◇ AQJxx   ♣ KQxx

Bid 2 ◇. You have neither an 18-point hand nor a real two-suiter. If partner bids again, you will show spade support. If he cannot bid again, you are quite willing to subside.

♠ Kxx   ♡ x   ◇ AQJxx   ♣ AQxx

Bid 2 ♣. You expect to raise spades at your next opportunity. You have 16 points in high cards, good 3-card spade support, and a singleton. This provides the 18 supporting points promised by your bid.

♠ x   ♡ Kxx   ◇ AQJxx   ♣ AQxx

Bid 1 NT. This is a choice of evils. You are unwilling to bid two clubs because you have neither a real two-suiter nor an 18-point hand. You avoid a rebid of two diamonds because that would suggest a *minimum* unbalanced opening bid. The rebid of 1 NT describes your high card strength accurately but gives a poor picture of your distribution. It is most unlikely that your partner will be seriously misled.

♠ Jx   ♡ Kxx   ◇ AQJxx   ♣ AQx

Bid 2 ♣. You expect to bid 2 NT at your next turn, showing a hand not quite strong enough for the immediate jump to 2 NT. Partner will go on to game with 7 or 8 points. If your second bid were 1 NT, showing 15 to 17 points, partner would tend to pass with only 7 or 8 points; if your second bid were 2 NT, showing 19 or 20 points, partner would tend to go on to game with 5 or 6 points. This method of bidding takes care of the skimpy 18-point hand or the well-fleshed 17-point hand.

OPENER	RESPONDER
1 ◇	1 ♠
2 ♣	?

♠ xxxx   ♡ xxx   ◇ Axx   ♣ Qxx

Bid 2 ◇. You don't expect to make a game, but it would be foolish to drop partner at two clubs where, for all you know, he may have only three cards.

♠ Kxxxx   ♡ xxx   ◇ Axx   ♣ xx

Bid 2 ♠. By all means give partner encouragement if he has the 18-point hand with good 3-card support for your major suit. If he raises to three spades, you will go on to game in spades!

♠ Qxxx   ♡ KQx   ◇ Kxx   ♣ xxx

Bid 2 NT. This shows 10 or 11 points in high cards and adequate strength in the unbid major suit.

♠ KJxx   ♡ KQx   ◇ Kxx   ♣ Qxx

Bid 2 ◇. Let partner clarify the nature of his hand. You expect to bid 3 NT at your next turn.

♠ xxxxx   ♡ KQxx   ◇ Kx   ♣ xx

Bid 2 ♡. If partner bids three clubs next, you will take him back to three diamonds. If he bids 2 NT, you will go on to 3 NT. If he bids two spades, you can go on to three spades, leaving it up to him to decide whether to pass, bid four spades, or bid 3 NT.

♠ xxxx   ♡ Axx   ◇ Kxxx   ♣ Qx

Bid 2 ◇. If partner bids 2 NT, you will raise to 3 NT. If partner bids two spades, you will go back to three diamonds. If partner bids three clubs (showing a real two-suiter) you will raise to *four* diamonds.

SUMMARY

When the bidding is opened with one of a minor suit, the opener will have either an unbalanced hand or a *strong* balanced hand.

With the unbalanced hand, opener will rebid his suit at his second or third turn to speak. With the strong balanced hand, opener will usually bid notrump at his second or third turn.

Responder's first duty is to show a major suit if he has one. He may feel secure in bidding even a very weak 4-card suit, for opener will not raise without four-card trump support.

If opener's second bid (or third bid) is in notrump, responder can use simple arithmetic to choose between a game and a part score.

If opener's second bid is one of a suit, responder bids 1 NT with 8 points or less; goes to the level of two with 8 to 11 points (the 8-point hand may go either way); and makes a forcing bid with 12 points or more.

Responder's immediate raise of the minor suit to *two* is forcing, promising 9 points or more. The immediate raise to *three* is pre-emptive, promising five or more trumps and not more than 8 points in high cards (usually less).

VARIATION

Weak Notrump Response: The response of 1 NT to an opening bid of 1 ♣ or 1 ◇ may be used to show a *maximum* of 8 points in high cards, with no four-card major suit.

This is safe, since opener must have at least 15 points if his distribution is balanced or a rebid in a minor suit if his distribution is unbalanced.

Chapter 6

Free Bids

The previous chapters have covered most of the essentials of Offensive Bidding—the various types of Opening Bid and the handling of subsequent auctions. However, except in the discussion of bidding sequences following the weak notrump opening, nothing has been said about the effect of enemy competition. After the opponents overcall an opening suit bid, do all responses and rebids remain the same in meaning?

Obviously not. If partner opens one club and you hold

♠ x x   ♡ Q J x x   ♢ K x x x   ♣ x x x

you will respond one heart. After all, opener may have a 20-point hand or tremendous support for hearts, and you will miss a game if you pass him out without giving him the chance to describe his hand with a rebid. But if your opponent overcalls one club with one diamond you will pass gratefully. Opener will now have his opportunity to speak again without a bid from you.

Similarly, if you open one spade with

♠   A K 10 x x   ♡ K x x   ♢ Q x x   ♣ x x

and partner responds 1 NT, you will rebid two diamonds. You want to give responder a chance to clarify his 1 NT bid—he may have a spade fit or a long heart suit. But if your opponent overcalls 1 NT with two clubs, you will pass. Your partner will have his chance to rebid anyway.

So the very nature of the game of bridge creates a difference in meaning between "forced" bids and "free" bids. Forced bids are made when a pass might end the auction, and may be intended only to give partner another chance to speak. Free bids are made when partner would have his chance regardless. They are prompted not by duty but by strength—the free bidder has substantial values which he actively desires to show. Let us see how free bids fit in with the rest of our system.

AFTER 1 ♠ OR 1 ♡

Strong Responses

The responses to a major-suit opening are not changed very much by an opponent's overcall. Strong responses, particularly, are hardly affected at all.

Suppose the opening bid is one spade and the opponent overcalls with two clubs. If responder intended to bid 2 NT or three spades or two hearts or two diamonds without the overcall, he can still do so. He must have a strong hand to make these bids whether they are "free bids" or not. However, responder will occasionally have to bid his suit at the three-level instead of the two-level, for the overcall may be in a suit higher-ranking than his own.

One real change is that a new strong bid is available—the penalty double.

Responder must remember that the penalty double is a *strong free bid*. He should not double merely because he has a lot of trumps and is sure that the opponents will be set. After all, the double may be taken out either by an opponent or by opener. Now, responder's hand must be rich enough in high cards to sustain a high contract of his own or to double the enemy in a different suit.

Here are some typical strong free responses. The auction goes:

PARTNER	OPPONENT	YOU
1 ♠	2 ◇	?

♠ xx   ♡ AJ10xxx   ◇ x   ♣ Axxx

Bid 2 ♡. You are strong enough to bid a new suit at the two-level, so the fact that you must bid freely does not change your action in any way.

♠ AJxx   ♡ Kxx   ◇ xx   ♣ Axxx

Bid 3 ♠. Just as if there were no intervening bid.

♠ Ax   ♡ xx   ◇ xx   ♣ KQJxxxx

Bid 3 ♣. Without the overcall you would have bid 2 ♣, but now you must go to the three-level.

♠ xx   ♡ AJx   ◇ K10xx   ♣ AJxx

Double. You would have jumped to 2 NT otherwise, but now you can take advantage of the overcall to make a penalty double. The set should be more than the value of your game if partner stands for the double. And if he doesn't, you can still go to 3 NT. (Incidentally, if opener takes out your double by bidding 2 ♠, the minimum rebid of his suit, you must PASS! *This means he has a psychic opening bid.* Partner must jump to three spades or bid a new suit if he wishes to take out your double when he has a legitimate opening.)

> ♠ xx   ♡ Qxx   ◇ KQ10xxx   ♣ xx

Pass. This hand is not strong enough in high cards for the double—a free bid. You can stand no other contract. Of course, if opener reopens the auction with a takeout double, you will be delighted to pass for penalties.

Weak Responses

What happens if partner opens one heart or one spade and an opponent overcalls when you were about to make a weak response—a 1 NT response or a single raise?

If you were going to raise, do it regardless. The free raise (1 ♠—2 ◇—2 ♠) is identical in limits and in meaning to the raise without the overcall. This is because a raise is not merely a "courtesy" bid to keep the auction alive; a raise is a bid you really want to make. It will enable opener to compete for a partial, bid a game, or take a sacrifice, knowing that you have trump support and a weak hand. Thus the requirements for a free raise and the auctions that follow it are the same as those described in Chapter 3.

On the auction:

OPENER	OPPONENT	YOU
1 ♠	2 ♣	?

> ♠ Kxx   ♡ xx   ◇ Q10xxx   ♣ xxx

Bid 2 ♠. This is a descriptive bid, telling partner you have a spade fit and a weak hand; and it is a pre-emptive bid, making it difficult for your left-hand opponent to show his values.

With most of the hands which call for a 1 NT response to a major-suit opening, you will pass if there is an intervening bid. The 1 NT response to one heart or one spade means that there is no game unless opener has extra values.

And if he has a strong opening he will bid again himself despite your pass. Normally, when you would have responded 1 NT there is nothing that you are eager to bid, so you do not bid freely.

On the auction:

OPENER	OPPONENT	YOU
1 ♡	2 ♣	?

♠ Qxx   ♡ xx   ◇ AJxxx   ♣ Jxx

Pass. Except for the overcall you would have responded 1 NT to give opener a chance to rebid with a very strong hand. Now he has that chance anyway.

There are, however, exceptional hands with which you will bid freely even though you would have responded only 1 NT had the opponents remained silent. One type is a weak hand containing a long suit, like

♠ xx   ♡ KJ10xxxx   ◇ xx   ♣ xx

If partner opens 1 ♠, you respond 1 NT, intending to bid hearts at your next turn. But suppose your opponent intervenes with two diamonds over one spade. You are still much too weak to bid two hearts directly, and yet it is wrong to pass when you have something you really want to bid. So you jump to *three* hearts. *The jump shift, when made as a free bid, is not a very strong bid, but a very weak one.*

On the auction:

PARTNER	OPPONENT	YOU
1 ♡	1 ♠	?

♠ xx   ♡ x   ◇ KQ10xxxx   ♣ Jxx

Bid 3 ◇. This bid is both descriptive and pre-emptive. It may inhibit the enemy from reaching their best contract.

If the free jump in a new suit is pre-emptive, what do you do when you want to suggest a slam or to check for a psychic opening? Here you use the strongest free bid of all, the cue bid of the enemy suit (1 ♠—2 ♣—3 ♣). Actually, it is because the opponent's overcall has made the cue bid available that the jump shift has been liberated for use with weak hands.

If partner's opening is psychic, always a strong possibility when you are responder with a mountainous hand and an opponent overcalls, over your cue bid he will make a minimum rebid—in his suit or in notrump whichever is cheaper—to deny a legitimate opening.

OPENER	RESPONDER
♠ K J x x x	♠ A Q x x
♡ x x x	♡ K Q 10 x
◇ x x	◇ A K Q
♣ x x x	♣ x x

OPENER	OPPONENT	RESPONDER	OPPONENT
1 ♠	2 ♣	3 ♣	Pass
3 ♠	Pass	4 ♠	Pass
Pass	Pass		

Opener's three-spade rebid definitely confirms a psychic, so responder contents himself with game. Note that the cue bid of three clubs has nothing whatever to do with responder's club holding.

Another exceptional case occurs when partner opens one heart and you hold a hand like

♠ K J x   ♡ x x   ◇ A J x x   ♣ J 10 x x

with which you intend to respond 1 NT and rebid 2 NT over opener's next bid. If over the one-heart opening your opponent overcalls one spade, you should respond 1 NT anyway. The free response of 1 NT is made with about 10 points, a balanced hand, and the opponent's suit securely stopped.

There is one last type of hand with which you would respond 1 NT to partner's major-suit opening, but bid freely over an overcall. This is the upper-level raise; you were planning to respond 1 NT to opener's bid of, say, one spade and to jump to three spades over his rebid. For example:

♠ K J x x   ♡ A 10 x x   ◇ x x   ♣ Q x x

What do you do with this hand when partner opens one spade and your right-hand opponent overcalls two diamonds? With 11 points in support of spades, you are 2 points too heavy for a two-spade free raise, and 2 points too light for a three-spade jump. So you must follow through with your original intention and bid notrump before raising spades. In this case, you will have to bid 2 NT, not 1 NT, but since you were willing to go as high as three spades anyway, this is no deterrent.

Your free 2 NT response is forcing on partner, who will make the identical rebid—one level higher—that he would have made over 1 NT had there been no opposition bidding. If opener rebids three spades he shows a six-card suit and you will raise him to four spades. If he rebids three clubs or three hearts, you bid three spades, clarifying the nature of your 2 NT response. Opener can go on to game or drop three spades, according to his strength.

OPENER	RESPONDER
♠ Q 10 x x x	♠ K J x x
♡ x x	♡ A 10 x x
◊ A Q x	◊ x x
♣ K J x	♣ Q x x

OPENER	OPPONENT	RESPONDER	OPPONENT
1 ♠	2 ◊	2 NT	Pass
3 ♣	Pass	3 ♠	Pass
Pass	Pass		

Responder shows a "2½" spade raise, but opener has minimum values and stops short of game.

In the specific instance where the opening bid is one heart and the overcall one spade, you still have the 1 NT response available. Here, with

♠ x x   ♡ K J x x   ◊ A 10 x x   ♣ Q x x

you will respond freely with 1 NT, and then jump to three hearts just as if there had been no overcall.

Of course, both this free 1 NT response and the free 2 NT response can also have their natural meanings—responder may be looking for a 3 NT contract. Opener cannot know until responder rebids whether his partner has a notrump type hand or has a strong supporting hand. However, responder's rebid will make the nature of his hand crystal clear.

Note that opener need have no qualms about raising the free 1 NT response to 2 NT, or the free 2 NT response to 3 NT. If responder has a notrump hand, fine. And if responder has a strong raise of opener's major, he will support it now.

FREE REBIDS BY MAJOR-SUIT OPENER

The same basic principles of free bidding apply as well to *opener's* free rebids. After you have opened in a major suit, you bid again freely only if there is some feature of your hand that you are anxious to describe—a powerful suit, extra high card strength, a long side suit. Virtually all of opener's rebids have the same general meaning whether or not there is an overcall. But, obviously, you will tend to have the maximum of the range described when the rebid is free, for otherwise you would have had no strong desire to make the bid. For example, unless the opponents acted, your rebid would be the same with both of these hands.

a. ♠ A K J x x   ♡ x x   ◇ A Q x x   ♣ x x
b. ♠ A Q x x x   ♡ x x   ◇ A J x x   ♣ x x

YOU	OPPONENT	PARTNER	OPPONENT
1 ♠	Pass	1 NT	Pass
2 ◇			

But suppose your opponent puts in a two-club bid over partner's 1 NT response. Now, you would still bid two diamonds with hand "a." However, with hand "b" you would pass. Unless partner can take independent action you are better off out of the auction. Likewise, with these two hands:

a. ♠ K Q 10 x x x   ♡ A x x   ◇ A x   ♣ x x
b. ♠ Q x x x x x   ♡ A J x   ◇ A x   ♣ x x

YOU	OPPONENT	PARTNER	OPPONENT
1 ♠	Pass	1 NT	Pass
2 ♠			

You would rebid two spades over 1 NT with either hand. But if your opponent overcalled after partner's 1 NT response, you would bid freely with hand "a" but pass with hand "b."

A similar situation prevails when it is opener's *left*-hand opponent who overcalls:

1 ♠	2 ♣	Pass	Pass
?			

Opener's rebid in this position is not, strictly speaking, a free bid, for if he passes the auction is over. But opener will be willing to end the auction with a pass unless he has some additional values, so here also he bids only when he really wants to.

The point is that responder has failed to make a free bid. So responder cannot have three cards or more in opener's major suit, for he would then have raised. He cannot have a good hand or a strong suit, for he would then have bid freely. He cannot have even a long suit in a weak hand, for he would then have jumped in his suit. Clearly, if opener has a minimum hand like

♠ KJxxx   ♡ Axx   ◊ KJx   ♣ xx

he can pass with complete assurance that he is missing nothing but trouble.

Of course, if opener's hand is better than a minimum, he will reopen the auction. The manner in which he reopens is dictated by his reason for acting. If he is reopening because he has a long, strong major suit, opener bids his suit:

1 ♠	2 ♣	Pass	Pass
2 ♠			

If because he has another long suit he has not yet shown, opener bids his second suit:

1 ♠	2 ♣	Pass	Pass
2 ♡			

If because he has substantially more than a minimum in high cards—15 points or more—opener doubles:

1 ♠	2 ♣	Pass	Pass
Double			

Note that this reopening double promises high card strength, not length in the opponent's suit. Responder is expected to take the double out to his best suit, or to return to opener's major. However, if responder himself has length in the opponent's suit but was too weak to double freely, he may pass opener's "takeout" double for penalties.

Here are some examples of reopening the bidding as opener. In each of the following hands, you have opened the bidding one spade; your left-hand opponent has overcalled two clubs; partner and right-hand opponent have passed. What do you do?

♠ A K J 10 x x   ♡ A x x   ◇ x x   ♣ x x

Bid 2 ♠. This hand may well "belong" to your side for a partial in spades if partner has a smattering of high cards. And if he hasn't, your fine suit provides insurance against disaster.

♠ A J x x x   ♡ x x   ◇ A Q 10 x x   ♣ x

Bid 2 ◇. Partner does not fit your spades well, but diamonds might be your spot. You have only a minimum in high cards, but two suits provide some safety, for it is very likely that partner can stand one of them.

♠ A K J x x   ♡ A Q x   ◇ Q 10 x   ♣ x x

Double. Whenever it is your strength, not your distribution, that prompts you to reopen, use the "takeout" double.

♠ A Q x x x x x   ♡ A x   ◇ K Q x   ♣ x

Bid 3 ♠. You are strong enough in high cards to double, but with a seven-card suit you would hate to hear partner pass the double for penalties. You bid three spades, not two spades, so that partner will know that any feature of his hand which will provide a trick for you might be enough to make game.

♠ K Q J x x   ♡ Q x   ◇ A x x x   ♣ x x

Pass. You have a minimum hand, and neither your spade suit nor your diamond suit is long or strong enough to provide safety opposite a partner who could not bid freely.

AFTER A MINOR-SUIT OPENING

Auctions that start with an opening bid of one club or one diamond are altered much more sharply by an enemy overcall than are those opened in a major suit. There are two reasons for this.

1. If your partner opens one spade, any suit response you make—two clubs, two diamonds, two hearts—is a strong bid, and you will bid your suit with or without an overcall. However, if partner opens one club, your suit

responses—one diamond, one heart, one spade—show only length in the suit bid, not strength. Now an overcall may have a great effect, for when made as free bids, these suit responses to a minor opening must show strength as well. So there are many hands with which you would respond one spade to partner's one-diamond opening if your opponent passes, but with which you would be too weak to bid if your opponent intervenes. In contrast, there are no hands which call for a two-diamond response to partner's one-spade opening with which you would be unwilling to bid freely.

2. The minimum opening in a major suit is much weaker than the minimum minor-suit opening. As we have seen, a major-suit opener will frequently allow his opponent to buy the contract with his overcall

| 1 ♠ | 2 ♣ | Pass | Pass |
| Pass | | | |

when he has no extra values. *This almost never happens when the opening bid is in a minor*. A minor-suit opener has either a strong balanced hand or a fairly strong unbalanced hand—his strength or his distribution is sure to provide a rebid. In other words, the extra strength required to open in a minor suit provides the incentive to reopen the auction.

Clearly, then, responder is under no pressure to bid freely when an opponent overcalls a one-club or one-diamond opening; he will get another chance even if he fails to bid directly. So responder should make the free bid only when he believes that there is a strong likelihood of game. Actually, this does not mean that he needs a powerhouse—the minor suit opening is normally a very sound hand, and responder can have visions of making game even when he himself has considerably less than an opening bid.

When should you, as responder, consider that game is likely? Assume that opener has a balanced hand too strong for a weak notrump—like a 16-point "strong" 1 NT opening. If you want to be in game opposite this strong notrump, you may bid freely at the one level. For example:

♠ A K J 10 x   ♡ x x x   ◊ x x x   ♣ x x

If partner opens one club and right-hand opponent overcalls one diamond, you will bid one spade. Eight points with a very strong five-card major suit is the very least you can have for the free bid. Likwise, with

♠ KJxx ♡ Qxx ◇ Jxx ♣ Kxx

you would make the free one-spade bid on the same auction. Ten points is the rock-bottom minimum when you have a four-card major and a flat hand. Note that in each of these examples you have the lightest hand with which you could ever commit your partnership to game over a "strong" 1 NT opening bid.

Let us see how the auctions develop after these free bids when partner has the balanced, and when he has the unbalanced, minor-suit opening.

OPENER		RESPONDER	
♠ Qx		♠ AKJ10x	
♡ Axxx		♡ xxx	
◇ K10x		◇ xxx	
♣ AQJx		♣ xx	

OPENER	OPPONENT	RESPONDER	OPPONENT
1 ♣	1 ◇	1 ♠	Pass
1 NT	Pass	2 ♠	Pass
2 NT	Pass	3 NT	Pass
Pass	Pass		

The two key bids in this sequence are opener's and responder's second bids. Opener rebids 1 NT over the free one spade response to show that he has a balanced 15-17-point hand with a diamond stopper. (With less than 15 points, opener would have started with a weak NT not one club; with more than 17 points, opener would rebid 2 NT not 1 NT; without a diamond stopper, for example, with

♠ Qxx ♡ AQJx ◇ xx ♣ AKxx

opener would bid two spades, not 1 NT, for to raise a major suit bid freely, he does not need four trumps.)

Responder's rebid is two spades, to show a minimum free bid that was predicated on his strong suit. (With more in high cards, responder could bid 3 NT; with better distribution he could bid a new suit or jump to three spades.)

Opener can pass two spades if he has a 15-point minimum and a poor spade fit. Here, however, he has 16 points, a fitting card in spades and a secure diamond stopper, so he goes on. Since both opener and responder have made strong bids, *any bid by opener over two spades is forcing to game.*

OPENER		RESPONDER	
♠ x x		♠ A K J 10 x	
♡ A J x x		♡ x x x	
◇ x		◇ x x x	
♣ A Q J x x x		♣ x x	

OPENER	OPPONENT	RESPONDER	OPPONENT
1 ♣	1 ◇	1 ♠	Pass
2 ♣	Pass	2 ♠	Pass
Pass	Pass		

Again, the rebids are the crux of the auction. Now opener has an unbalanced minor-suit opening, so he rebids two clubs. (He would have to be at least an ace stronger to rebid two hearts, a "reverse" that is forcing to game over a free bid.) Opener's hand is not severely limited by this two-club rebid, which is forcing on responder. The bid shows an unbalanced, but not necessarily a minimum opening.

Responder has the same light free bid based on strong spades, so he rebids two spades. In this instance, opener is happy to pass, for he has no extra values. But many other actions are available to opener at this point. In general, his bid here will place the final contract; opener knows almost exactly what responder holds.

OPENER		RESPONDER	
♠ Q x		♠ K J x x	
♡ A x x x		♡ Q x x	
◇ K 10 x		◇ J x x	
♣ A Q J x		♣ K x x	

OPENER	OPPONENT	RESPONDER	OPPONENT
1 ♣	1 ◇	1 ♠	Pass
1 NT	Pass	2 NT	Pass
3 NT	Pass	Pass	Pass

Opener shows a balanced 15-17-point hand with his 1 NT rebid. Responder shows a minimum balanced free bid by rebidding 2 NT. (With an extra point or two, or with a five-card suit, responder would jump to 3 NT.)

Opener would pass 2 NT if he held a flat minimum with a poor spade fit. Here, of course, he goes on.

OPENER	RESPONDER
♠ xx	♠ KJxx
♡ AJxx	♡ Qxx
♢ x	♢ Jxx
♣ AQJxxx	♣ Kxx

OPENER	OPPONENT	RESPONDER	OPPONENT
1 ♣	1 ♢	1 ♠	Pass
2 ♣	Pass	3 ♣	Pass
Pass	Pass		

As in the earlier example, opener rebids two clubs to indicate his unbalanced distribution. Responder is forced to bid, as opener may have a much better hand. But since responder has a minimum free bid, he makes the minimum raise of opener's suit. (If responder were a little stronger, he could jump in clubs, bid a new suit, or, with a diamond stopper, bid 2 NT.)

Opener passes three clubs with his minimum opening bid. But with extra values he could try for game.

So far we have considered only free bids in major suits at the one-level. These are the most common free bids after a minor-suit opening, but many others are possible. For example, raises and jump raises of opener's minor suit. These free raises retain the identical meaning and limits that they have without the overcall. The single raise is strong and forcing; the jump raise is weak and preemptive.

Likewise, the free jump to 2 NT is the same 12-14-point balanced hand as it is without an overcall. Of course, the stopper in the enemy suit must be certain.

Then there is the free response of 1 NT. This shows a balanced hand of 10 or 11 points with the opponent's suit solidly stopped. For example, you might hold

♠ KJx   ♡ Qxx   ♢ KJx   ♣ xxxx

for the auction: 1 ♣—1 ♢—1 NT. Note that the hand contains no four-card major, for responder would bid it in preference.

The jump shift changes into a weakness bid when used freely (1 ♣—1 ♢—2 ♠) over a minor, as well as over a major, opening. Here again the cue-bid ($1 \clubsuit$—$1 \diamondsuit$—$2 \diamondsuit$) is available for the very powerful hands, leaving the jump in a new suit for worthless hands that contain long suits. Responder must never employ this jump bid if his hand might produce game opposite the fairly strong balanced hand, for opener will pass the jump when he holds the 15-17-point hand. On the auction:

OPENER	OPPONENT	YOU
1 $\clubsuit$	1 $\diamondsuit$	?

♠ QJxxxxx   ♡ xx   ◇ xx   ♣ xx

Bid 2 ♠. You are not worried about missing game, for opener needs a very powerful hand to bring in four spades. The hand very probably belongs to the enemy. But with

♠ KQJxxxx   ♡ x   ◇ xxx   ♣ xx

Bid 1 ♠. You would bid 4 ♠ over a "strong" 1 NT opening, so this hand qualifies for a free bid of one spade.

The free response of two clubs after a one-diamond opening ($1 \diamondsuit$—$1 \heartsuit$—$2 \clubsuit$) is unaffected by the overcall. It is always a bid that responder wants to make, so if he intended to bid two clubs without the overcall, he will do so freely.

However, all the other nonjump free responses at the two-level: $1 \clubsuit$—$1 \spadesuit$—$2 \diamondsuit$; $1 \clubsuit$—$1 \spadesuit$—$2 \heartsuit$; $1 \diamondsuit$—$1 \spadesuit$—$2 \heartsuit$ become *extremely* strong bids. This is because these bids are in higher-ranking suits than opener's. Opener, with an unbalanced hand, must rebid his suit at the three-level, and the partnership may well find itself contracting to take 10 tricks before it can sign off. Therefore, these free responses at the two-level are virtually forcing to game—responder must be able to envision game opposite an unbalanced minimum. On the auction:

OPENER	OPPONENT	YOU
1 $\clubsuit$	1 $\spadesuit$	?

♠ xx   ♡ KQxxx   ◇ AJxx   ♣ xx

Pass. You would want another king to make a free two-heart bid. You will get a second chance to bid your heart suit later in the auction. Remember, partner will not pass out one spade.

OPENER'S FREE REBIDS

As a general rule, after a minor-suit opening, opener's free rebids have the identical limits that the bids would have were there no overcall. In this example:

OPENER	OPPONENT	RESPONDER	OPPONENT
1 ♣	Pass	1 ♡	1 ♠
1 NT			

the free rebid of 1 NT still means 15-17 points and a balanced hand. But since opener now has the option of passing without ending the auction once there is an overcall, his free rebids are likely to be near the maximum of the range described. That free 1 NT rebid, for example, is probably 16 or 17 points with good spades.

With both of the following hands you should open one diamond and rebid two diamonds over partner's one-heart response:

a. ♠ xx   ♡ xx   ◇ AKJxx   ♣ KQxx
b. ♠ x   ♡ xx   ◇ AKJxxx   ♣ KQxx

However, if your right-hand opponent overcalls one spade (1 ◇—Pass—1 ♡—1 ♠), you should pass with hand "a" but bid two diamonds freely with hand "b." Note that in neither case dare you rebid two clubs, which would show a very much stronger holding.

If you intended to jump to three diamonds over one heart with, say,

♠ xx   ♡ Qx   ◇ AKQJxx   ♣ AQx

you would still do so if your opponent intervenes. Jump bids are not affected by an overcall—they are always bids which you are eager to make.

Likewise, any time you were going to raise partner's suit, you will raise freely if there is an overcall. Obviously, the raise too is one of the rebids you really want to make, not one you make only to keep the auction alive. In fact, there are hands with which you support partner's suit freely when you would have rebid in notrump without the overcall.

This comes about when the overcall denies you the 1 NT rebid. The opponent's bid may be at the two-level (1 ◇—Pass—1 ♡—2 ♣), and even if it is at the one-level (1 ◇

—Pass—1 ♡—1 ♠) you may not have the solid stopper in the enemy suit required for a free 1 NT rebid. For example, if you open the bidding with one club, holding

♠ Q x   ♡ A Q x   ◇ Q 10 x   ♣ A Q 10 x x

you intend to rebid 1 NT if partner responds one heart, reserving the raise in hearts for later in the auction. However, if your opponent overcalls with one spade (1 ♣—Pass—1 ♡—1 ♠) you can no longer rebid 1 NT, for stronger spades are required. With such a fine hand you want to bid freely, so you support hearts directly.

Your action would be the same if the overcall were two diamonds, not one spade. You would still rebid two hearts. You have a diamond stopper but to rebid 2 NT freely, you need 18-19 points, not 15-17. Remember, the *free* raise of partner's suit does not promise four-card support. This is the only significant change in the meaning of opener's rebid after an overcall.

REOPENING THE AUCTION

When you have opened the bidding in a minor suit and your left-hand opponent's overcall has been passed around to you (1 ◇—1 ♡—Pass—Pass) you will almost always reopen the auction. The minor suit opening is never the bare minimum that might be opened one spade or 1 NT; it has a little extra, either in high cards or distribution.

If this "little extra" is in distribution, you will rebid your suit or bid a new suit. These bids promise no more than a minimum minor-suit opening.

For the very powerful opening bids you have the jump rebids, which are virtually unchanged in meaning. When you have "a little extra" in high cards, you make one of two strong rebids: Double or 1 NT. The difference between the two actions is that the double shows length in unbid major suits, while the notrump rebid shows strength in the enemy suit. On the auction:

YOU	OPPONENT	PARTNER	OPPONENT
1 ♣	1 ♠	Pass	Pass

♠ J x   ♡ A Q x x   ◇ K x x   ♣ A Q x x

Double. You are strong in high cards and have a substantial holding in hearts, the unbid major. But with

♠ A Q x x   ♥ J x   ♦ K x x   ♣ A Q x x

Bid 1 NT. This shows 15-17 points with good spades.

If you have one of these modestly strong hands, you may well have a cold game even though partner has not made a free bid.

YOU			PARTNER
♠ J x			♠ x x x
♥ A Q x x			♥ K J x x
♦ K x x			♦ A Q x x
♣ A Q x x			♣ x x

YOU	OPPONENT	PARTNER	OPPONENT
1 ♣	1 ♠	Pass	Pass
Double	Pass	3 ♥	Pass
4 ♥	Pass	Pass	Pass

Partner is not nearly strong enough for a free bid at the two-level, but when you reopen with a double, he knows that you have a strong hand with hearts. Therefore he jumps to three hearts to suggest game, an invitation you are happy to accept. Had partner the same hand but with a small diamond instead of the ace, he would bid two hearts and you would pass.

YOU			PARTNER
♠ A Q x x			♠ x x
♥ J x			♥ Q x x
♦ K x x			♦ A Q 10 x x x
♣ A Q x x			♣ x x

YOU	OPPONENT	PARTNER	OPPONENT
1 ♣	1 ♠	Pass	Pass
1 NT	Pass	3 NT	Pass
Pass	Pass		

Partner is too weak to bid two diamonds freely (and too strong for *three* diamonds), but when you reopen with 1 NT he knows just where he wants the hand to play. With one diamond fewer, he would raise to 2 NT instead of 3 NT.

OVER TAKEOUT DOUBLES

Up to now we have allowed the opponents to intervene in our auctions only with overcalls. What if the enemy enters the auction with a takeout double?

By and large, we handle opponent's takeout doubles by treating them just as if they were overcalls. That is to say, when responder bids a new suit over the double (1 ◇—Double—1 ♠, or 1 ♠—Double—2 ♣), *he is making a free bid*. He is not "running out" of the doubled contract; he is not "bidding weakness." Responder is making a strength-showing, *forcing,* free bid.

This is true whether the opening was in a major or in a minor suit. A free bid in a new suit over a double says, "Partner, this is what I was going to bid if your opponent hadn't doubled, *and I really wanted to bid it.*" For example, on the auction:

OPENER	OPPONENT	YOU
1 ♡	Double	?

♠ xx   ♡ xx   ◇ Axx   ♣ AKJxxx

Bid 2 ♣. This is the bid you would have made had your opponent passed. Do not let him distort your natural auction.

♠ KQxxxx   ♡ xx   ◇ Kxx   ♣ xx

Bid 1 ♠. You were going to respond one spade if there were no interference, and you were going to be happy to make the bid. Do it regardless.

On the auction:

OPENER	OPPONENT	YOU
1 ◇	Double	?

♠ AKxxx   ♡ xx   ◇ xxx   ♣ Qxx

Bid 1 ♠. You are strong enough for a free bid at the one-level, and you have a suit that you really want to bid.

♠ K10xx   ♡ xx   ◇ xxx   ♣ Qxxx

Pass. You would have responded one spade were there no double, but only to keep the auction alive.

A good illustration of our "natural" bidding over opponent's takeout doubles is this hand from the 1957 World's Championship Match: U. S. v. Italy.

♠ A 5 4	♠ K J 7
♡ K 9 6	♡ A Q 10 5 3
◇ Q	◇ 10 8 5
♣ K 10 6 4 3 2	♣ Q J

U. S.	ITALY	U. S.	ITALY
1 ♣	Double	Redouble	1 ♠
2 ♣	Pass	2 NT	Pass
3 NT	Pass	Pass	Pass

The auction given is that of one of the best "standard bidding" partnerships in America. Three notrump was defeated two tricks while the Italians, at the other table, easily bid and made four hearts. But our players were not at fault—their system was.

In standard bidding, responder could not bid one heart, for this is not forcing. So he had to distort the auction by first redoubling. Now, when it was next his turn, he had to choose between bidding his heart suit and showing his spade stopper—he could not do both. He made an intelligent decision, but was wrong.

How much simpler it is when the free bid in a new suit is played as forcing! Responder no longer need guess; he can show all his features in normal order.

As a rule, we employ the "redouble" only when we have a fit for partner's suit and intend to raise him. When partner's opening bid has been doubled by an opponent, you have four types of raise, graded according to strength.

1. *Redouble, then jump in opener's suit:*

OPENER	OPPONENT	RESPONDER	OPPONENT
1 ♠	Double	Redouble	Pass
Pass	2 ◇	3 ♠	

This is forcing to game. You have 13 points or more in support.

2. *Redouble, then support opener's suit:*

OPENER	OPPONENT	RESPONDER	OPPONENT
1 ♠	Double	Redouble	Pass
Pass	2 ◇	2 ♠	

This is invitational, but not forcing to game. You have 10 to 12 points in support.

3. *Jump raise of opener's suit:*

OPENER	OPPONENT	RESPONDER
1 ♠	Double	3 ♠

This is pre-emptive, and partner needs a strong hand to make game. You have 7 to 9 points in support.

4. *Single raise of opener's suit:*

OPENER	OPPONENT	RESPONDER
1 ♠	Double	2 ♠

This is a "courtesy" raise with 4 to 6 points in support, made mainly to embarrass the opponents.

Here are examples of each type of raise after partner's opening bid of one spade has been doubled:

1. *Redouble then jump:*

   ♠ A Q x x   ♡ x x   ◇ x x x   ♣ A Q x x

2. *Redouble then support:*

   ♠ A Q x x   ♡ x x   ◇ x x x   ♣ K x x x

3. *Jump raise:*

   ♠ A Q x x   ♡ x x   ◇ x x x   ♣ J x x x

4. *Single raise:*

   ♠ Q x x   ♡ x x   ◇ x x x   ♣ Q x x x x

These stepped raises apply to minor suits as well as to majors. Obviously, however, the trump length, as distinguished from overall strength, must be much greater to support a minor suit, where opener may have a three-card holding, than to support a major-suit, when opener promises a five-card suit.

Over an opponent's double, just as over an overcall, the free jump shift (1 ◇—Double—2 ♡, or 1 ♠—Double—3 ♣) is a pre-emptive, "weakness" bid. Whenever responder has a long suit but is too weak in high cards to make a free bid over the double, he can jump in his suit.

```
                        NORTH
                    ♠ Q J 10 x x x
                    ♡ x x
                    ◇ x
                    ♣ J x x x
        WEST                        EAST
    ♠ A x x                     ♠ x
    ♡ Q x x                     ♡ K x x
    ◇ A Q x x x                 ◇ K J x x
    ♣ K x                       ♣ Q 10 x x x
                        SOUTH
                    ♠ K x x
                    ♡ A J 10 x x
                    ◇ 10 x x
                    ♣ A x
```

SOUTH	WEST	NORTH	EAST
1 ♡	Double	2 ♠	3 ♣
3 ♠	Pass	Pass	Pass

Sitting North-South, we bid and made three spades on this deal, taken from a recent team match. At the other table, our partners bid and made five diamonds with the East-West cards. Their auction:

SOUTH	WEST	NORTH	EAST
1 ♡	Double	1 ♠	2 ♣
Pass	2 ◇	Pass	4 ◇
Pass	5 ◇	Pass	Pass
Pass			

Here East-West had an easy time, whereas against us West would have had to bid his diamond suit for the first time at the four-level. Once again, our policy of *keep the auction low with strong hands, but get it up high in a hurry with weak hands* paid off handsomely.

VARIATIONS

Non-Forcing Double Raise: The non-forcing double raise (described at the end of Chapter 3) is not affected by an opponent's overcall at the level of two.

OPENER	OPPONENT	RESPONDER
1 ♠	2 ◇	3 ♠

The jump to three spades is still non-forcing, just as though the overcall had not been made. Responder would jump to 3 NT to show the values for a *forcing* raise in opener's major suit.

Not so, however, when the overcall is at the level of three:

OPENER	OPPONENT	RESPONDER
1 ♠	3 ◇	3 NT

The response of 3 NT must be assigned its natural meaning since this may be the best game contract and the partnership must have some way of reaching it and staying there.

Responder may bid 3 ♠, as usual, to show four trumps and 10 or 11 points in support of spades (perhaps even such three-card support as Q-x-x). With slightly more, responder should jump to *four* spades. With substantially more than 15 points in support of the opening bid, responder may bid a new suit or make a cue-bid in the opponent's suit, after making due allowance for the strength shown by the opponent and the possibility that the opening bid was psychic.

Negative Doubles: After a minor-suit opening and an overcall by the next player, responder may double to show enough strength to compete. The "negative" double denies the values or the suit-length needed for a free bid.

OPENER	OPPONENT	RESPONDER
1 ♣	1 ♡	Double

Responder should have four spades with about 8 to 11 points in high cards. With more than four spades, he should bid rather than double; with fewer, he can usually find a raise or a notrump response. A typical hand for the double:

♠ Kxxx   ♡ xx   ◇ AQxx   ♣ xxx

Opener should pass the negative double only when he has unusual length and strength in the opponent's suit. The purpose of the double is to make it easier for the opener to bid—particularly in an unbid major suit.

Opener should respond logically and naturally to the negative double. If he has opened with a minimum hand and a rebiddable suit, he merely rebids his suit. If he has opened with a balanced hand of 15 to 17 points, he responds in notrump or an unbid major. With stronger hands, he can make a jump bid in his original suit, a new suit, or notrump; or he may cue-bid in the opponent's suit to show strength and a willingness to let responder pick the suit.

When responder *fails* to double the next player's overcall, he may have either a very bad hand or the values for a penalty double rather than a negative double. If the overcall is passed around to the opener, he may decide whether or not to reopen the bidding.

In general, opener should pass when he has merely a long minor suit in a hand of minimum value. Opener should double for takeout when he has 15 points or more, with good support for at least one unbid suit; there is a fair chance that responder will be glad to pass the double for penalties. Opener should avoid a rebid of 1 NT with 15 or a thin 16 points and strength in the opponent's suit; partner's silence indicates a hand too weak for a negative double, and the opener may be well out of the auction.

Responsive Doubles: When your partner doubles the opening bid for takeout, and the next player raises the opening bid, you may double to show that you have strength but no clear-cut action.

SOUTH	WEST	NORTH	EAST
1 ◇	Double	2 ◇	Double

East may have some such hand as:

♠ J x x x   ♡ Q x x x   ◇ x x x   ♣ K x

East does not want to guess which major suit to bid. He will pass West at two hearts or two spades, but will raise if West jumps to three of a major.

If East has a somewhat better hand, say the ace of clubs instead of the king, he can double two diamonds "responsively" with the intention of raising two of a major to three. And if East has slightly more than that, he may double and then raise West's major suit to game.

The responsive double may be used, also, when partner overcalls (instead of using a takeout double). The double then shows good support for the two unbid suits.

SOUTH	WEST	NORTH	EAST
1 ◇	1 ♡	2 ◇	Double

East shows support for the two unbid suits (spades and clubs in this case), but a hand lacking the strength or the type of suit needed for a bid in a new suit.

It is customary for the partnership to agree on a cut-off point for responsive doubles, beyond which any double is for penalties. For example, they may agree to use responsive doubles through 3 ♡ and penalty doubles of 3 ♠ or any higher bid.

Chapter 7

Slam Bidding

YOUR OBJECT in slam bidding is to get to all of the slams that can be made by reasonable play of the cards, and to stay out of the slams that will go down.

In practice, this is an impossibly high standard. Some slams depend not on the cards held by your side but on the distribution of the cards held by the opponents. For example, you may justifiably bid a slam that is defeated only because one opponent holds all four of the outstanding trumps; the odds are 9 to 1 against so bad a break.

You will be content to get to most of the slams for which you have an even chance or better. You want to stay out of slams for which you have less than an even chance. You are willing to get to a slightly worse slam on rare occasions, just as you are willing to miss an odds-on slam on rare occasions. But it should not be necessary for you to miss many good slams or to bid many bad slams.

Most slams depend on one of three factors:

1. *Power:* You have so many high cards that you have a good play for the slam even without a long suit. The opponents don't have enough high cards to take the first two tricks, and they may be no great threat at any stage of the play. In general, you need about 33 points in high cards to enjoy this dominant position at a small slam contract; or 37 points at a grand slam.

2. *Long Suit and Controls:* You have enough winners in one or two long suits to assure twelve tricks, provided that the opponents cannot defeat you by winning the first two tricks. You don't need 33 points, but you do need aces in at least three suits, with a king or singleton in the fourth suit. The Blackwood Convention is likely to be very useful for this type of slam.

3. *Short Suits and Fit:* You have one or two very strong suits, supplemented by at least one singleton or void suit. You expect to make the slam with ruffing tricks as well as long suits and high cards, and you may achieve this with far less than 33 points in high cards—perhaps even less than 26 points!

161

Slams that can be made on sheer power are the easiest to bid. The other types often require two other essential ingredients: a sensible bidding system, and sensible bidders.

The bidder must have the sense to see that a slam is possible under certain conditions (the right controls, the right fit, or whatever). He must then select the bids that will describe his hand or that will persuade his partner to furnish a description.

The bidding system must make it possible for the sensible bidder to do his work. Even the most delicate and imaginative bids are useless if your partner has no way of knowing what you mean by them.

We are now ready to see how slams are bid in our (eminently sensible) system.

AFTER AN OPENING BID OF 1 NT

The opening bid of 1 NT promises 12 to 14 points with balanced distribution. Responder may bid a slam on sheer power if he has 21 points, for the combined count will then be 33 to 35 points. Responder may bid a grand slam on sheer power if he has 25 points or more, for then the combined count will surely be 37 points or more.

The responder has a problem with hands of 19 or 20 points with 4-3-3-3 distribution. Such hands will make a slam if the opener has 14 points or even a good 13 points; they are unsafe at slam if the opener has only 12 points. Responder solves the problem by jumping from 1 NT to 4 NT.

This is just a raise (as we will soon see, there is another way of finding out about aces) rather than a conventional bid, and is clearly a slam try. Responder would show a long suit if he had one instead of making such a bulky bid. The hand should be safe for ten tricks even if the combined count is only 31 points.

After the raise to 4 NT, opener bids slam with 14 points, but passes with 12 points. He uses his judgment with 13 points.

Responder is sometimes in position to bid a long-suit slam immediately, provided only that opener has enough aces. In order to find out about the aces, responder jumps immediately to four clubs (the Gerber Convention).

The Gerber four-club bid (which we use only as an immediate response to 1 NT or 2 NT) asks opener to indicate how many aces he has:

Bid	Number of Aces
4 ♦	none or all four *
4 ♡	one
4 ♠	two
4 NT	three

After receiving information about aces, the responder may find out about kings by bidding five clubs. The information is given in the same way, one level higher.

♠ x   ♡ K Q J x x x x x   ◇ A Q J   ♣ x

Bid four clubs in response to an opening bid of 1 NT. If opener has no aces, you will bid four hearts next and play the hand there. If opener has one ace, *he* will bid four hearts, and you will pass! If opener has two aces, he will bid four spades, and you will bid six hearts; the slam may depend on a diamond finesse. If opener has three aces, you will still bid six hearts; you will surely lack the king of diamonds, for partner cannot have a king as well as three aces.

Responder may have some sort of two-suiter instead of a freakish one-suiter. If so, he jumps to four clubs only if he needs no help in determining the eventual trump suit.

When responder needs help in picking the trump suit, he customarily jumps to three of the higher suit (provided that at least one is a major suit) and proceeds with a rebid in the other suit, with the Blackwood Convention, with a cue bid, or even with a direct jump to slam.

OPENER	RESPONDER
1 NT	3 ♡ (1)
4 ♡ (2)	4 NT (3)

(1) Forcing to game. Opener is asked to bid 3 NT if he has only two hearts. With three or more hearts, opener

---

* Opener cannot have all four aces for an opening bid of 1 NT; but may have all of them for an opening bid of 2 NT.

In order to bid 4 ♣ in response to 1 NT, responder needs a hand that is safe at 4 NT or five of a suit if opener has the *wrong* number of aces; and that will make a slam if opener has the *right* number of aces. Responder's hand is usually a freakish one-suiter with nothing but kings or singletons in the side suits. Responder should not have a void, because then he is not dependent solely on aces; nor any weak suit of two or more cards, since then information about aces will not solve his bidding problem.

must bid four hearts or a new suit. Opener bids a new suit *on the way to four hearts* to show that he has three or more hearts, good values for the opening bid, and some substantial high-card strength (usually an ace) in the suit being shown at this stage. If responder has no interest in slam, he simply bids four hearts and ends the matter.

(2) Opener has three or more hearts and obeys orders. Apparently, opener does not have a maximum in top cards since has has neglected to bid a new suit.

(3) Blackwood, despite opener's pessimism.

Responder should have some such hand as:

♠ x   ♥ A K J x x x   ♦ A K Q x x   ♣ x

As long as opener has three or more hearts, there should be a good play for slam if opener's hand includes one ace. A grand slam is doubtful even if opener shows two aces, for then he must surely lack the queen of hearts. (Opener would surely cue bid in response to three hearts if he had Q-x-x of hearts and two aces.) Nevertheless, it is worth noting that responder may have to consider a grand slam even though he knows that the combined count is only 29 to 31 points.

Most of the slams that begin with an opening bid of 1 NT are reached with the aid of a cue bid by opener:

OPENER	RESPONDER
1 NT	3 ♠
4 ♣	

Opener's rebid of four clubs is not a serious offer to play the hand at any number of clubs. Responder has asked him to bid four spades with three or more cards in that suit, but to bid 3 NT if he has only two spades. Any bid of a new suit by responder means that he is ready and willing to bid four spades and that he can afford to show something useful on the way to four spades.

When should opener make this kind of mild slam try? He can afford to do so with a maximum (14 points) if the hand includes a high trump and at least one ace. He may make the slam try with a minimum (12 points) if the hand includes a high trump and two aces.

The cue bid should show an ace. By way of exception, however, opener may cue-bid a suit headed by K-Q if his hand is good enough and if his only ace is in responder's bid suit.

Responder will usually be interested only in game. He will return to four of his suit, knowing that opener has a good fit for that suit. No harm has been done by the cue bid even if no good has come of it.

When responder does happen to be interested in slam, however, the cue bid may solve all of his problems—for or against the slam. For one thing, it is helpful to know that the notrump hand has good structure in aces and kings. Moreover, the ace may help responder's hand enormously—or it may warn him of fatal duplication of values.

For example, suppose responder has:

♠ A Q x x x x   ♥ none   ♦ K Q J x x   ♣ Q x

He bids three spades in response to 1 NT. If opener raises to four spades, responder should pass. If opener's rebid is 3 NT, responder should bid four diamonds in the hope that there is a slam in diamonds.

Let us suppose that the auction proceeds in a more encouraging vein:

OPENER	RESPONDER
1 NT	3 ♠
4 ♣	?

Apparently, opener has three-card spade support, the ace of clubs, and some reason to be optimistic. Responder should jump to six spades. The chances are very good that the spades are solid and that there will be a reasonable play for slam.

If opener's rebid were four hearts instead of four clubs, responder would give up the idea of bidding a slam, and would sign off at four spades. The ace of hearts is pretty useless opposite his hand, and he cannot afford much waste when he has only 14 points in high cards opposite a hand of 12 to 14 points. This would still be true if the responder's hand were slightly improved.

When the opener has more than one ace, he should make his cue-bid in the cheapest suit. This gives responder maneuvering space:

OPENER	RESPONDER
1 NT	3 ♥
3 ♠	4 ♣
?	

Responder is clearly interested in a slam, since otherwise he could sign off at four hearts. Opener is being given the chance to show another ace if he has one. He can bid four diamonds or even five clubs to show a second ace. With no further aces, opener can sign off at four hearts.

This is an additional reason for responder's discouragement with a rebid of four hearts in the case given earlier. If opener's lowest ace is the ace of hearts, the opponents must hold the aces of diamonds and clubs. Slam should be out of the question.

The same system of cue bids can be used even when opener lacks support for the first suit. For example:

OPENER	RESPONDER
1 NT	3 ♠
3 NT	4 ♢
?	

Opener may bid four spades to show a simple preference for spades. He will prefer diamonds with four cards in that suit, particularly if he has a doubtful stopper in one of the unbid suits. A raise to five diamonds would show some sort of four-card diamond holding with a hand that opener disliked for slam purposes. Opener may cue-bid in an unbid suit (four hearts or five clubs, in this case) to show an ace and some interest in slam in responder's second suit. Responder might then bid five or six diamonds, according to whether or not the cue bid excited his interest; or he might even bid four spades (over four hearts) in a renewed attempt to play the hand at game in that suit.

It will be seen that most of the slam tries made by this method occur below the level of game. If a fit is discovered, well and good; otherwise the partnership rests content with the normal game contract.

In competitive bridge, over the course of the last few years, we have found that slams bid by this method not only occur fairly frequently, but also account for large gains. Most partnerships simply don't have the tools to separate the slam from the nonslam hands when the combined high-card count is so meager.

After an opening bid of 1 NT, responder usually starts with the (Stayman) response of two clubs if he intends to try for a minor-suit slam. At his next turn he has his first chance to indicate that his interest is in the minors. (Responder cannot begin with a jump to three clubs or three diamonds, since both of these bids are pre-emptive.)

Consider this auction:

OPENER	RESPONDER
1 NT	2 ♣
2 ♠	3 ♣ (or 3 ♦)

Responder has too good (or too unbalanced) a hand to raise to 3 NT. He is interested in game at clubs or diamonds—which must mean that slam cannot be too far from his thoughts.

What should opener do when he discovers that his partner is interested in game or slam at a minor suit? He needn't do anything drastic, but he should revalue his hand for slam purposes. No matter that it counts only 12 to 14 points; partner is well aware of that fact and has still displayed some sort of slam ambition. Is there a fit for partner's minor suit? Is the weak notrump based on top cards (aces and kings) or on queens or jacks? Is the count nearer to 14 points than to 12 points?

If opener has a fit, top cards, and 14 points, he shows some enthusiasm for slam. If he has poor fit, few top cards, and only 12 points, he drags his feet. If he has a mixture of good and bad features, he must use his judgment.

OPENER	RESPONDER
1 NT	2 ♣
2 ♡	3 ♦
?	

♠ Axx ♡ AJxx ♦ Kxxx ♣ xx

Bid three spades. You have only 12 points in high cards, but the diamond support is fine, the top card structure is good, and the doubleton may be useful. Since it is known that you do not have a biddable spade suit, this is clearly a cue bid.

♠ xx ♡ AJxx ♦ Kxxx ♣ Axx

Bid four clubs. The same hand, with the suits switched. You are willing to go beyond 3 NT in encouraging your partner.

♠ xx ♡ AJxx ♦ Kxxx ♣ KQx

Bid four diamonds. You have only one ace, but the other top cards are pretty good. You cannot make a cue bid, but your willingness to go past 3 NT is significant.

♠ Q J x   ♥ K x x   ♦ K x x   ♣ K J x

Bid 3 NT. A poor hand for slam purposes. Sign off.

Responder may have some such hand as:

♠ K x   ♥ K x x   ♦ A Q 10 x x x   ♣ A x

Since he has only 16 points in high cards, he knows that the combined count is only 30 points at most. He needs a fit and controls, and can afford to do a bit of exploration.

If responder has a better hand, he will begin in the same way but may bid the slam even if he gets no encouragement from the opener.

AFTER AN OPENING BID OF 2 NT

The opening bid of 2 NT shows 21 or 22 points (or a magnificent 20 points), with balanced distribution and all suits stopped.

Responder can bid a slam on power if he has 12 to 14 points. With 15 points, he tries for a grand slam. With 16 points or more he makes sure of reaching a grand slam.

With 11 points and flat distribution, responder cannot be sure of a small slam. He solves the problem by jumping to 4 NT. (This is not a conventional bid, since responder jumps to four clubs—Gerber—to find out about aces.) Opener bids slam with 22 points but passes with 21 points.

The responder tries for the slams that depend on a long suit and controls by jumping to four of his long suit:

OPENER	RESPONDER
2 NT	4 ♠ or 4 ♥ or 4 ♦

This sort of bid is used in standard bidding systems but has its greatest value in the post mortem. If a slam is bid and made, responder preens himself on his jump response "which got us there." If a slam is bid and goes down, responder sadly points out that he didn't try for a slam; he just showed a good suit; he'd have bid the hand differently if he were interested in a slam. If a slam is made but not bid, responder sadly points out that he did *his* share; he made a jump bid, didn't he; he can't very well bid both hands, can he; and so on.

We prefer that a bid have its greatest value while the auction is still going on. It is possible to play such a jump to mean "Stop" or to mean "Bid again," but it must mean one and not one-or-the-other. In our system, the jump response to 2 NT is forcing for one round. Opener must bid 4 NT (Blackwood) whereupon the partnership discovers whether or not there is a slam.

What sort of hand should responder hold? He should have a long suit (six or seven cards) that is presumably solid if opener has K-x or A-x (or better); he should have one or more aces or kings on the side; and he should have no singleton or void.

The long suit and side high card should make him safe at a contract of five-odd. Since singletons or voids are not disclosed by the Blackwood Convention, responder should avoid insisting on a Blackwood bid when his response will not settle all of opener's problems.

OPENER	RESPONDER
♠ K J x	♠ A Q x x x x
♡ A J x	♡ K x x
◊ K Q x	◊ x x
♣ A K x x	♣ x x

OPENER	RESPONDER
2 NT (1)	4 ♠ (2)
4 NT (3)	5 ◊ (4)
6 ♠ (5)	Pass (6)

(1) Shows 21 or 22 points, etc.

(2) Demands a Blackwood rebid.

(3) Obeying orders.

(4) Showing one ace.

(5) Opener has a fine hand for slam purposes: a good fit for spades, and no suit in which the opponents may conceivably take the first two tricks.

(6) Only a confirmed hog would consider 6 NT. Slams that depend on a long suit and controls should usually be played in the suit.

Opener might have a different hand:

♠ K J x   ♡ Q J x   ◊ K Q J   ♣ A K Q x

He would discover, on using the Blackwood Convention, that the opponents held two aces. He would sign off at five spades, and responder would pass.

Responder is not powerless if he lacks the sort of hand just described. He may still get to a slam that depends on a fitting trump suit with a fit elsewhere as well.

OPENER	RESPONDER
2 NT	3 ♠
4 ◇	

This is a cue bid, made by the opener on his way to four spades. As in the case of the opening bid of 1 NT, opener tends to make a slam try of this kind with a good fit for responder's suit and high-card structure suitable for slam. He would content himself with a rebid of four spades if he had the fit for responder's suit without the appropriate strength in aces and kings. Opener would rebid three no-trump if he had only two spades, or even with a three-card spade holding if he had all suits doubly stopped and considerable strength in queens and jacks.

When the opener does cue bid, he shows his cheapest ace. In the example, opener indicates a good fit for spades, about 22 points with encouraging strength in aces and kings, the ace of diamonds—and no ace of clubs. So much information is conveyed by the cue-bid that responder can usually make an intelligent decision without further probing.

Responder may get good results with a mediocre two-suiter even when his first suit fails to strike a spark.

OPENER	RESPONDER
2 NT	3 ♠
3 NT	4 ◇
5 ♣	

This is a cue bid, made by the opener on his way to five diamonds. He should have a doubleton in spades, the ace of clubs, no ace of hearts (since he failed to make the cheaper cue bid of four hearts), and a slamworthy hand within the limits of the strength shown by his opening bid. Responder can hardly hope for a more complete picture.

The negative side of the picture is equally revealing, if less encouraging. Opener might bid four spades at his second turn to show a belated preference for spades. Or he might bid merely five diamonds to show diamond support with a hand that has a poor structure in aces and kings.

AFTER AN OPENING BID OF TWO CLUBS

As we have seen, the opening bid of two clubs shows either a very strong notrumper (23 points or more) or a hand that will probably produce a suit game opposite a bust. Opener will indicate at his second turn which type of hand he holds.

When the opening bid is the notrump type, it usually takes a positive response to pave the way to a slam. However, this is not always the case. Responder may bid two diamonds with a mess of queens and jacks, since these are not useful for slam at a suit. When opener bids notrump (at his second turn), responder may be able to bid a slam on sheer power.

OPENER	RESPONDER
2 ♣	2 ◇
2 NT	6 NT

Responder should have a count of about 10 points without any ace or king. For example:

    ♠ Q J x   ♡ Q J x   ◇ Q x x   ♣ Q J x x

Responder may have even less if the opener's second bid is *three* notrump, showing 25 or 26 points. Responder should bid a slam on any balanced hand of 8 points or more.

More often than not, however, the slam is bid after a *positive* response to the opening bid of two clubs. The opener still shows 23 or 24 points by making a minimum rebid in notrump. Most hands that begin in this way are bid to a slam.

OPENER	RESPONDER
2 ♣	2 ♠ (1)
2 NT (2)	5 NT (3)
6 ♠ (4)	Pass (5)

(1) This positive response promises about 8 points or more, with more than one quick trick.

(2) The balanced hand of 23 or 24 points, with all suits stopped. Opener may have good support for spades, but he can show this later.

(3) A general sort of slam bid, asking partner to choose the slam. In this case, the choice is between 6 NT and six spades.

(4) Opener has good support for spades, and probably a doubleton.

(5) Satisfied with partner's choice. Presumably responder has at least five spades. With a four-card suit, he would have bid 6 NT instead of 5 NT.

Responder should have some such hand as:

♠ A J x x x   ♡ K x x   ◇ Q x x   ♣ x x

The slam that depends on a long suit and controls may be bid in any of three general ways: Gerber by the responder; Blackwood by the responder, after he has bid two suits; and Blackwood by the opening bidder, after a jump rebid by responder.

OPENER	RESPONDER
♠ A x x	♠ K Q J x x x x
♡ K Q J x	♡ x
◇ A J x	◇ K Q x x
♣ A K J	♣ x

OPENER	RESPONDER
2 ♣ (1)	2 ♠ (2)
2 NT (3)	4 ♣ (4)
4 NT (5)	6 ♠ (6)
Pass (7)	

(1) The forcing opening bid.

(2) More than enough for a positive response.

(3) The balanced hand of 23 or 24 points, with all suits stopped.

(4) Gerber. How many aces, partner? (With a real club suit, responder could bid merely *three* clubs.)

(5) Three aces.

(6) No grand slam. Small slam is assured.

(7) A bid of 6 NT could not be criticized, particularly at match-point play.

OPENER	RESPONDER
♠ A x x	♠ K Q x x x
♡ A J x x	♡ x
◇ A x x	◇ K Q x x x
♣ A K Q	♣ x x

OPENER	RESPONDER
2 ♣ (1)	2 ♠ (2)
2 NT (3)	3 ◇ (4)
3 ♠ (5)	4 NT (6)
5 ♣ (7)	5 NT (8)
6 ◇ (9)	6 ♠ (10)
Pass (11)	

(1) The forcing opening bid.

(2) More than enough for a positive response.

(3) The balanced hand of 23 or 24 points, with all suits stopped. In this case, opener has only 22 points, but should count something extra for all four aces.

(4) Asking for a choice of suits.

(5) The choice.

(6) Blackwood. How many aces, partner?

(7) All four aces.

(8) Blackwood. How many kings, partner?

(9) Only one king.

(10) Responder cannot quite guarantee a grand slam unless opener has four-card support for one of the long suits. If opener has only A-x-x in each of the suits, the grand slam is no bargain (about an even money shot).

(11) Opener would bid the grand slam if he had A-x-x-x in either of responder's suits. As matters stand, however, opener has done his all.

OPENER	RESPONDER
♠ K x x	♠ A Q J x x x
♡ A x x	♡ K x x
◇ A K Q x	◇ x x
♣ A K J	♣ x x

OPENER	RESPONDER
2 ♣ (1)	2 ♠ (2)
2 NT (3)	4 ♠ (4)
4 NT (5)	5 ◇ (6)
5 NT (7)	6 ◇ (8)
7 NT (9)	

(1) The forcing opening bid.

(2) More than enough for a positive response.

(3) The balanced hand of 23 or 24 points, with all suits stopped.

(4) Similar to the jump response over an *opening* bid of 2 NT. Opener must now bid 4 NT (Blackwood).

(5) Obeying orders.

(6) One ace.

(7) Blackwood. How many kings, partner?

(8) One king.

(9) Opener can count 13 tricks.

When the three methods are compared, it will be seen that the responder uses Gerber when he has a freakish one-suiter. Responder uses Blackwood when he has a good two-suiter. Responder forces opener to use Blackwood when he has a good but balanced one-suiter.

There is, in addition, a fourth method:

OPENER	RESPONDER
2 ♣	2 ♠
2 NT	3 ♠
4 ♦	

This is, quite clearly, a cue bid on the way to four spades. If responder is interested, he goes on; if not, he can stop at game. The situation is quite similar to those already described in the treatment in this chapter of slam bidding after an opening bid of one and two notrump.

As usual, the negative inference is just as useful as the positive.

OPENER	RESPONDER
2 ♣	2 ♠
2 NT	3 ♠
3 NT or 4 ♠	

Opener is not interested in a slam. If he bids 3 NT, he should have only two spades. If he goes to four spades, he should have three-card support. In either case, his bid is in the nature of a sign-off.

Responder may go on with a further slam try or with a jump to slam if he has the hand for such strong action. If his interest in a slam is, however, quite tentative, the sign-off may head him away from an unsafe venture to the level of five-odd.

When the opening bidder has the *suit* type of two-club bid, he bids his suit at his second turn. From here on, the bidding is much the same as though the opener had opened with a forcing bid of two in his best suit in Standard American Bidding.

Slam is seldom bid when the first response is negative. Slam is often bid when the first response is positive. The opener will usually show his suit first, and will use the Blackwood Convention later. Occasionally, he will show his suit and then bid other suits in the attempt to find a fitting high card in a particular suit. In such case, the failure to use the Blackwood Convention suggests a void suit.

OPENER	RESPONDER
2 ♣	2 ♡
2 ♠	3 ♠
4 NT	

Here the opener has a game-going hand with a long spade suit. As soon as partner shows values and spade support, the opener uses the Blackwood Convention. Probably, the opener intends to bid a small slam in any case and is trying to find out whether or not a grand slam is a good risk.

OPENER	RESPONDER
2 ♣	2 ♡
2 ♠	3 ♠
4 ♢	4 ♠
5 ♢	

Apparently, the opener has a tremendous two-suiter. Responder is encouraged to attach special value to high cards in diamonds. The chances are that he can disregard top cards in hearts. Opener's failure to use the Blackwood Convention indicates that he is not interested in aces in general, but only in *particular* high cards.

OPENER	RESPONDER
2 ♣	2 ♡
2 ♠	3 ♠
4 ♢	4 ♠
5 ♣	

Opener almost surely has a void in hearts. He has the aces of clubs and diamonds, and is trying to find out how good the fit is. Responder should discount top cards in hearts but should attach extra value to high cards in clubs and diamonds. Specifically, responder should bid five diamonds or six clubs to show the king of such a suit; should bid five hearts to warn partner that his top cards are in that suit; and should sign off at five spades if he has no particular message to convey.

AFTER A MAJOR-SUIT RAISE

Probably the most common of all slam sequences begins with a double raise of the opening major suit:

OPENER	RESPONDER
1 ♠	3 ♠

The situation is the same as in Standard American Bidding. Opener may try for a slam with a bid of 4 NT (Blackwood) or with a cue bid (any new suit).

Correct procedure has been described in most of the standard bidding books. We need only point out that opener should use the Blackwood Convention only when the crucial information is the number of aces held by responder. There is no excuse for asking a question when the answer does you no good. It is especially important to avoid using Blackwood when you have a worthless doubleton in an unbid suit.

A cue bid is a try for slam but may be extremely tentative. Opener may have only the mildest interest in a slam, and may intend to come to an abrupt halt unless he gets enthusiastic encouragement. Responder should avoid getting past game unless he has the material for enthusiasm: maximum values for the double raise (about 15 points), good high card structure in aces and kings, and good distribution.

Responder's return to the agreed trump suit is a sign-off:

OPENER	RESPONDER
1 ♠	3 ♠
4 ◇	4 ♠

Opener should pass if he has only a vague interest in slam. He should go on, however, if his interest in slam is real and specific.

For example, opener may now cue-bid a new suit:

OPENER	RESPONDER
1 ♠	3 ♠
4 ◇	4 ♠
5 ♣	

Obviously, opener needs help in the fourth suit; if he had a control in that suit he could bid the slam all by himself. Responder should bid five hearts to show the ace of that suit, and should jump to six spades if he has second-round control of the unbid suit. (Alternatively, responder may bid 5 NT to indicate that he has the king of the unbid suit and is willing to play the hand at slam in notrump.) Responder signs off at five spades if he has neither first nor second-round control in the unbid suit.

A special meaning is attached to a repeated cue bid in the same suit:

OPENER	RESPONDER
1 ♠	3 ♠
4 ◇	4 ♠
5 ◇	

In most partnerships, this sequence has no definite meaning. It is possible that opener is *telling* that he has both the ace and the king of diamonds. It is equally possible that the opener is *asking* if his partner has help in diamonds. Either method is playable, provided only that the partners understand which is being used.

In our opinion, asking is more important than telling in this situation. A player who has the ace and king of the same suit can usually find something else to show or may be able to use the Blackwood Convention. The player who needs help in a specific suit has only this way of finding out what he wants to know. We therefore recommend our method (although it is not an integral part of the system) of using this repeated cue bid to ask partner to bid a slam with help in the cued suit (king or ace, or singleton with unusual trump length) but to stay out of slam with only small cards in the cued suit.

Opener would use this method with some such hand as:

    ♠ AQJxx   ♡ none   ◇ Axxxx   ♣ AJx

Slam is a good gamble if partner has help in diamonds, but a bad gamble if partner has three small diamonds even if his hand is otherwise remarkably good.

Responder would bid a slam if he had:

    ♠ Kxxx   ♡ xx   ◇ Kxx   ♣ KQxx

and it would be ice cold. He would also bid the slam with:

    ♠ Kxxx   ♡ KQxx   ◇ Kxx   ♣ xx

in which case the club opening lead would beat the contract. However, these are 12-point hands, and even the slightest improvement would make the slam an odds-on shot.

The same principles apply when it is responder's suit that has been raised:

OPENER	RESPONDER
1 ◇	1 ♠
3 ♠	

Responder may use Blackwood or may make a cue bid in a new suit. A return to opener's suit would be a slam try but would not necessarily show the ace. It would indicate good support and would hint that slam is likely if opener really has length instead of only a three-card suit.

As we have seen, the double raise in this situation shows 18 or 19 points in support of a major suit, with four or more trumps. Responder should consider a slam with anything that looks like an opening bid, say 12 points or more. With 15 points or more, responder's interest in slam should be keen and lively.

Responder needs more when the raise is only single:

OPENER	RESPONDER
1 ◇	1 ♠
2 ♠	

Here, the opener has four trumps with 15 to 17 points. Responder begins to think about slam with 15 points (or an exceptionally fine 14-point hand). In this situation, responder may make a cue bid in a new suit but will subsequently have to make another cue bid to make it clear that he is thinking of slam rather than merely game.

OPENER	RESPONDER
1 ◇	1 ♠
2 ♠	3 ♣
3 ♠	4 ◇ or 4 ♡

Responder is clearly trying for a slam. His first rebid of three clubs might have been a mere game try, but he would have no reason to bid four diamonds or four hearts if he were just trying to reach game; he could simply bid four spades. Hence he is now trying to reach a slam, which means that even his first rebid was a slam try.

A middling position is occupied by the systemic auction:

OPENER	RESPONDER
1 ♦	1 ♠
2 ♣	2 ♦
2 ♠	

As we have seen, this sequence shows good three-card support, with a total of 18 points in support of spades. Responder may now proceed with a slam try if he has about 13 points or more, provided that he is satisfied with three-card trump support.

Responder must beware of confusing the single raise after a minor suit with the single raise after a major suit. In this auction:

OPENER	RESPONDER
1 ♡	1 ♠
2 ♠	

Opener does *not* have four trumps with 15 to 17 points. He has a minimum opening bid (about 13 to 15 points) with spade support that may be as poor as x-x-x.

It is important to remember that, in the system, the following auction is forcing to game:

OPENER	RESPONDER
1 ♠	2 ♣
2 ♠	3 ♠

Responder has a club suit, fair three-card support for spades, and a hand that should produce a game opposite an opening bid. If he had four-card support for spades, he would almost invariably be able to bid three spades at his first turn.

Opener may bid merely two spades at his second turn with a very fine hand, since responder guarantees a rebid. Having discovered that responder has spade support, opener may now move towards a slam.

Because of the forcing nature of the previous auction, a special meaning can be attached to this similar auction:

OPENER	RESPONDER
1 ♠	2 ♣
2 ♠	4 ♠

There is no need for responder to jump to four spades just to reach game. This auction should be reserved for hands that have exceptional strength and length (9 or 10 cards) in the two bid suits. Opener is invited to go to slam if he controls both of the unbid suits. If he controls only one of the unbid suits, he may make a cue bid in the hope that his partner's singleton is in the other unbid suit.

OPENER	RESPONDER
♠ A Q J x x	♠ K x x x x
♡ A Q x	♡ x x
◇ x x	◇ x
♣ x x x	♣ A K Q x x

OPENER	RESPONDER
1 ♠	2 ♣
2 ♠	4 ♠
5 ♡	6 ♠
Pass	

If opener has both red aces, he would bid 4 NT and later 5 NT in an attempt to make responder bid the grand slam. If opener had the ace of one red suit and the king of the other, he would bid six spades at his third turn instead of making a cue bid.

If responder had the wrong singleton he would bid only five spades at his third turn. The opponents, presumably, would take the first two tricks in the unbid suit.

AFTER A MINOR-SUIT RAISE

Many fine minor-suit slams are reached after the strong single raise of a minor-suit opening:

OPENER	RESPONDER
1 ♣	2 ♣

If opener really has his minor suit, not a three-carder in a strong balanced hand, he can confirm his suit, show extra values, and indicate some feature of his hand all at the same time by bidding a new suit over partner's raise. This lays a firm base for slam investigation—a suit has been established, both partners have shown strength, and you are only at the two-level.

Consider this hand which we bid together in a national team championship some years ago:

OPENER	RESPONDER
♠ A x x	♠ x
♡ K x	♡ A x x
◇ Q x x	◇ K J x x x
♣ A K 10 x x	♣ Q x x x

OPENER		RESPONDER	
1 ♣		2 ♣	(1)
2 ♠	(2)	3 ◇	(3)
3 NT		4 ♣	(4)
4 ◇	(5)	4 ♡	(6)
6 ♣	(7)		

(1) The strong single raise is preferable to a bid of one diamond with a strong unbalanced hand.

(2) "I have a real club suit, a strong hand, and some spade feature, likely the ace."

(3) Now responder shows his side suit.

(4) "If you bid two spades because you were worried about notrump, so am I; if because you are interested in slam, so am I."

(5) Opener shows his diamond fit.

(6) Responder cue-bids his heart control.

(7) Opener confidently bids the odds-on slam.

This hand resulted in a tremendous gain for our team, for in the other room our opponents' auction was simpler but less accurate:

OPENER	RESPONDER
1 NT	3 ◇
3 NT	

Three notrump was down one while six clubs was made easily.

AFTER A JUMP TAKEOUT

Responder's jump takeout is a slam try:

OPENER	RESPONDER
1 ♡	2 ♠

Responder thinks there may be a slam even if the opening bid is a minimum. He should have excellent support for opener's suit, or an independent suit of his own, or (rarely) overwhelming strength in high cards. Except where the strength is so overwhelming that responder will eventually bid a slam on sheer power, the responding hand should include at least two aces.

Opener should rebid as normally as possible. When the vulnerability is unfavorable, so that a psychic opening bid may be ruled out, opener may make any rebid that describes his hand. In other vulnerability conditions, opener must avoid the rebid that indicates a psychic opening bid. Except for this restriction, opener rebids his suit to show length and strength, bids notrump to show scattered strength and balanced distribution, bids a new suit if he has one, or raises responder's suit with Q-x-x or better.

At his second turn, responder clarifies the nature of his hand. He may raise opener's suit, rebid his own suit, or bid notrump, depending on which of the three types of hand he holds.

Sometimes a raise of opener's suit does not do justice to the hand. In such cases, responder may mark time by bidding a new suit, after which he will raise the opener's suit. This sequence of bids guarantees a singleton in the responder's unbid suit.

OPENER	RESPONDER
1 ♡	3 ♣
3 ◇	3 ♠
3 NT	4 ♡

Responder should have some such hand as:

    ♠ A x x   ♡ Q J x x   ◇ x   ♣ A K J x x

Improve the hearts to K J x x, and responder's third bid should be five hearts rather than merely four. Improve the hand still further:

    ♠ A Q x   ♡ K J x x   ◇ x   ♣ A K J x x

and responder's third bid should be *six* hearts. In this case, he is clearly interested in a grand slam.

THE DELAYED RAISE

The delayed raise just illustrated is one of the most powerful of all slam tries. It occurs in many different sequences, always indicating that the delaying bid is a cue bid, hinting at slam.

OPENER	RESPONDER
1 ◇	1 ♡
1 ♠	2 ♣
2 NT	4 ♠

Obviously responder could have raised spades at his second turn. Why did he mark time with a bid of two clubs? It wasn't clear at the time, since he might have had a real club suit or might have been showing a stopper for notrump purposes. But when responder comes out from behind the bushes with the spade raise, it is clear that the club bid was meant to show an ace. Moreover, responder must have a singleton in his unbid suit. (This is not necessarily true if responder never jumps, but a player who bids three suits, including a jump bid at any stage, guarantees a singleton in the fourth suit.)

How does this differ from the related auction:

OPENER	RESPONDER
1 ◇	1 ♡
1 ♠	3 ♣
3 NT	4 ♠

In this case, responder has jumped in clubs rather than in spades. He still shows four-card spade support and a singleton in his unbid suit. He still has a fine hand. The difference is that he has very powerful clubs and only moderately good spades when he jumps in clubs; but has very powerful spades and only moderately good clubs when he makes the nonjump bid in clubs and the jump in spades.

For the jump in spades, responder might have:

 ♠ KQxx ♡ KQxxx ◇ x ♣ Axx

For the jump in clubs, however:

 ♠ Qxxx ♡ KQxxx ◇ x ♣ AKx

As we have seen, the same principle is observed in the case of reverse bids. In all such situations, the partner is strongly urged to go on, but is allowed to stop short if the fit is wrong.

COMPETITIVE BIDS

The jump takeout is pre-emptive when the opponents are in the auction:

OPENER	OPPONENT	RESPONDER
1 ♡	1 ♠	3 ◊

If the responder has the very powerful hand, he must cue-bid in the opponent's suit. In this case he would bid two spades instead of three diamonds.

This must be taken as a guarantee of strong support for opener's suit. If responder has an independent suit of his own, he should bid it without jumping, unless he can afford to make the cue bid and later a jump bid in his own suit.

A delayed cue bid is sometimes a slam try and sometimes an attempt to get to game in notrump.

SOUTH	WEST	NORTH	EAST
1 ♡	1 ♠	2 ◊	Pass
2 ♡	Pass	2 ♠	

This is an attempt to get to three notrump. North has other, unmistakable ways of trying for slam if he needs them.

SOUTH	WEST	NORTH	EAST
1 ♡	1 ♠	2 ◊	Pass
2 ♡	Pass	3 ♡	Pass
3 ♠			

A cue bid, hinting at slam. South is unlikely to be interested in notrump, since a fit has been found in a major suit. If he were interested, he would simply bid notrump himself at this point.

It is sometimes possible to ask partner whether or not he can control the first or second round of the opponent's suit:

SOUTH	WEST	NORTH	EAST
1 ♡	1 ♠	2 ◊	Pass
2 ♡	Pass	3 ♡	Pass
5 ♡			

South asks his partner to bid a slam if he can take the first or second spade trick. South should have good hearts, a fit for diamonds, and the ace of clubs:

♠ x x   ♡ A K J x x x   ◊ K J x   ♣ A x

North should raise to six hearts with any hand that includes the ace, king, or singleton in spades.

The same principle may be used for the unbid suit if the opponents are not in the auction:

OPENER	RESPONDER
1 ◇	1 ♡
1 ♠	3 ♠
5 ♠	

Responder is asked to bid six spades if he has ace, king, or singleton in the unbid suit. Opener should have some such hand as:

♠ KQxx   ♡ Ax   ◇ AKQxx   ♣ xx

Sometimes an opponent gets into the auction only by way of a penalty or lead-directing double of a cue bid. Over such a double, a pass is the weakest possible action; a redouble shows king or singleton (assuring partner that he need not worry about this suit if slam is bid in a different suit); a raise of the doubled suit shows a void; and a free bid shows strength of some kind but denies ability to redouble or raise the doubled suit.

An example, from the 1957 Summer National Team Championships:

KAPLAN	SHEINWOLD
♠ AJ105	♠ KQ84
♡ Q63	♡ 10
◇ AJ10642	◇ KQ5
♣ None	♣ QJ864

KAPLAN	OPP'T	SHEINWOLD	OPP'T
1 ◇	Pass	1 ♠ (1)	Pass
2 ♠ (2)	Pass	3 ♣ (3)	Double
4 ♣ (4)	Pass	4 ◇ (5)	Pass
4 ♠ (6)	Pass	5 ♡ (7)	Pass
6 ♠ (8)	Pass	Pass	

(1) The four-card major is bid rather than the mediocre five-card minor.

(2) Promises four-card spade support and 15 to 17 points. In this case, 12 points in high cards and 5 points for the void.

(3) A slam try. Sheinwold intends to raise diamonds next in the hope of suggesting the shortness in hearts or of prying some information out of his partner.

(4) Guaranteeing complete control of the suit—void, or singleton ace.

(5) Sheinwold has decided to bid a slam but sees no harm in further exploration. There may be a grand slam if Kaplan has a void in clubs and the other three aces. Furthermore, somebody may double six spades if the bidding sounds confused.

(6) Signing off. If he is being asked for a high heart, he simply doesn't have it.

(7) The grand slam is out of the question, since Kaplan would have been happy to bid four hearts if he had three aces and a void. Sheinwold makes one further attempt to coax a penalty double from the enemy.

(8) Confirming the quality of his trumps. If Kaplan had bid only five spades, however, Sheinwold would have gone on to six. The opponents did not double, but their team mates stopped at five diamonds at the other table.

The slam was bid with only 25 points in high cards in the partnership hands. But for the opponent's double, it might have been impossible to reach the slam. This illustrates the folly of doubling a cue bid unless you have the most compelling of reasons. In this case, the doubler was due to lead against a spade contract and had no need to make a lead-directing double.

Since many opponents are guilty of such folly, it pays to be ready with a way of profiting by their mistakes. One hand of this sort may decide a match.

VOID RESPONSE TO BLACKWOOD

Our way of showing a void in response to a Blackwood 4 NT bid, although not an integral part of the system, pleases us better than any other we have seen.

The situation arises only when you have agreed on a trump suit, your partner bids a Blackwood 4 NT, and you have at least one ace and a void suit. If you have opened the bidding or made a jump takeout you are entitled to make the void-showing bid only if you have two aces and a void; in all other situations, you need only one ace and a void.

If you are entitled to make the void-showing bid, jump to six in the void suit if that suit is lower than the agreed suit. Otherwise jump to six in the agreed suit.

OPENER	RESPONDER
1 ♡	3 ♡
4 NT	?

Responder bids six clubs to show one ace and a void in clubs; six diamonds to show one ace and a void in diamonds; six hearts to show one ace and a void in a suit higher than hearts (obviously spades).

OPENER	RESPONDER
1 ◇	2 ♠
3 ◇	4 ◇
4 NT	?

Responder jumps to six clubs to show *two* aces and a void in clubs; but jumps to six diamonds to show two aces and a void in a suit higher than diamonds (obviously hearts). The advantage of locating the void is that your partner may be able to bid a grand slam.

Chapter 8

Defensive Bidding

STRICTLY SPEAKING, Defensive Bidding—auctions that start with an opponent's opening bid—is not an integral part of our system. All our offensive bidding stems logically and inevitably from our concept of opening bids; clearly this cannot be the case when our opponents open the auction. But defensive bidding is a field which has virtually been ignored by bridge authorities, and we have strong views on the subject to present here.

The basis of standard defensive bidding is a dim, unformulated theory that when an opponent opens the bidding you should "double" for takeout with almost any strong hand, and overcall if you have merely a fair hand. Consider these four examples:

a. ♠ x   ♡ Qxxx   ◇ AQJxx   ♣ Qxx
b. ♠ x   ♡ Axxx   ◇ AQJxx   ♣ Qxx
c. ♠ xxx ♡ xx   ◇ AQJxxx   ♣ Kx
d. ♠ Axx ♡ xx   ◇ AQJxxx   ♣ Kx

Suppose your opponent opens one spade and you are next to speak. With hand "a" you overcall two diamonds in standard bidding, since you are too weak to make a takeout double. However, with hand "b" you double since now you are strong enough. Hand "c," once again, calls for the overcall. But hand "d" is too strong for a mere two-diamond bid—you must double.

Now this leads to a great deal of confusion and difficulty, for it is impossible for the doubler's partner to evaluate his hand. In standard bidding, what should you do when partner doubles an enemy one-spade opening bid and you hold

♠ xxxx   ♡ KJxxx   ◇ Kx   ♣ xx

You should jump to three hearts if your partner holds hand "b":

♠ x   ♡ Axxx   ◇ AQJxx   ♣ Qxx

for you want to be in game, yet he will pass if you bid only two hearts. But if partner holds hand "d" instead:

♠ A x x   ♡ x x   ◇ A Q J x x x   ♣ K x

you had better bid two hearts, not three hearts, since you are probably too high even at the two-level. How can you determine whether or not you have a good hand for partner when you have no way of knowing what pattern hand he holds? And if you make the minimum forced response with all sorts of hands, waiting to hear a clarifying rebid from partner, how can he tell whether you have a Yarborough (so that he must pass to avoid a bad penalty) or have two kings and a five-card major suit (so that it is safe for him to bid again)? Through using the double for strong hands regardless of pattern and the overcall for slightly weaker hands, standard defensive bidding has become a guessing game.

We, however, approach defensive bidding differently. With us, *pattern,* not strength, is what distinguishes the takeout double from the overcall. Our guiding principle is simple: *We overcall when we have a good idea of what suit to make trump. We double when we think the hand should play in partner's best suit.* Both double and overcall have fairly wide ranges of strength. Just as with an opening major-suit bid, a hand's distributional pattern determines the initial bid, its strength determines the rebid. Let us take another look at those four examples. With both "a" and "b"

a. ♠ x   ♡ Q x x x   ◇ A Q J x x   ♣ Q x x
b. ♠ x   ♡ A x x x   ◇ A Q J x x   ♣ Q x x

we would double, not overcall, an opponent's one-spade opening bid. These hands have an excellent pattern for a takeout double—shortness in the enemy suit and length in all the others, including fine support for the unbid major suit. Nothing about these hands suggests that diamonds is the suit to make trumps. In fact, the prime chance for game with either hand is in hearts.

Is it not dangerous to double one spade with so weak a hand as "a"? Not at all! It is far safer than to overcall. If you overcall two diamonds and are doubled, you may be in for a severe penalty, and neither you nor your partner can know whether or not there is a better spot. However, if you double instead of overcalling, even if you catch partner with a weak hand, you have the considerable extra chance of finding a snug harbor in hearts or clubs. You have nearly tripled your margin of safety.

With examples "c" and "d"

c. ♠ x x x   ♡ x x   ◇ A Q J x x x   ♣ K x
d. ♠ A x x   ♡ x x   ◇ A Q J x x x   ♣ K x

we would overcall two diamonds, not double one spade. Now it is likely that the hand will play best in *our* suit, not in a suit we force partner to bid. Of course, if partner has a long, strong suit of his own, he can bid it voluntarily over our overcall. But otherwise, the pattern of these hands suggests that diamonds (or notrump) should be our final contract.

Is there not an appreciable danger of missing game by bidding "only" two diamonds with "d"? No, for partner knows that an overcall may be made with a powerful hand, and he will keep the auction alive if he has a smattering of high cards. He will not pass a two-diamond overcall with any of these hands:

♠ x x   ♡ 10 x x x   ◇ K x x   ♣ A x x x
♠ x   ♡ x x x x   ◇ 10 x x x   ♣ A J x x
♠ Q 10 x   ♡ K 10 x x   ◇ x x   ♣ Q J x x

But if partner will bid over our overcalls with such light hands, is it not dangerous to overcall with a hand like example "c"? Yes, it is. Hand "c" is a doubtful, dangerous overcall of two diamonds—only the quality of the suit, which provides some safety, makes it acceptable. Without the ◇ J, the bid would be unthinkable. As it is, we would pass with hand "c" over a one-spade opening if we were vulnerable.

As we have seen, overcalls are much more dangerous than takeout doubles and so cannot be made so freely. When we have a really strong hand, we can enter the auction after an enemy opening bid with either an overcall or a double, according to our pattern. But when we have only a moderately strong, borderline hand, we tend to pass unless our distribution is suitable for a takeout double.

THE TAKEOUT DOUBLE

We have already indicated the features which make a hand suitable for a takeout double. These are 1) support for all three unbid suits, with particular emphasis on length in the unbid major suits, and 2) moderate to great high-card strength. In our view, the first feature—hand pattern—is by far the more important. If compelled to double an opening bid of one spade with one of these two hands:

1. ♠ x   ♡ Qxxx   ◊ Qxxx   ♣ Qxxx
2. ♠ KQxx   ♡ x   ◊ Axx   ♣ AQxxx

we would choose to double with Hand 1 which has the ideal pattern, rather than with Hand 2 which has a wealth of high cards. To illustrate this, suppose that partner has the hand we discussed earlier:

♠ xxxx   ♡ KJxxx   ◊ Kx   ♣ xx

and jumps to three hearts when we double one spade. If we have doubled with Hand 2, we are in for serious trouble despite our quite respectable point-count—the least that can happen to us is to be set two or three tricks in four clubs doubled. And this is all loss, as the enemy probably cannot make even a partial.

But if we have doubled with Hand 1, we are perfectly safe in three hearts. True, we can be doubled there and set from one to three tricks. However, the opponents can certainly make game in spades and possibly even slam. So we cannot lose, and may show a substantial profit, by playing in three hearts doubled.

This is the magic of "fit"—when you and your partner have eight or nine trumps between you and a short suit or two in one hand or the other, no harm can come to you through buying the contract no matter how the high cards are divided. If the opponents have most of the high cards you will be taking a profitable sacrifice, for if you have good fitting hands so have the enemy. And if your side has the balance of power you will fulfill your contract. This is why takeout doubles are so safe when you have the right distributional pattern—if partner fits one of your three suits, you cannot be hurt.

Of course, we do not suggest that you make takeout doubles with only three queens in your hand. Pattern is more important, but you cannot ignore your point count. Unless minimum high-card standards are set up, partner will never be able to tell whether the hand "belongs" to your side or to the enemy. The decision to double an opponent's opening bid is predicated on both pattern and strength.

The basic distributional requirement for the takeout double is that you have at least three cards in each unbid suit. So the pattern ranges from the barely acceptable 4-3-3-3 to the perfect 5-4-4 with a void in the opponent's suit. The closer your pattern is to the ideal, the less you need in high cards. To express this in terms of points, count shortness in the enemy suit as if you were a supporting hand—add 1 point for a doubleton, 3 points for a singleton, 5 points for a void. If your opponent opens one heart, value your hand for a double as if you were supporting spades, the unbid major suit. For example,

♠ A J x x   ♥ x   ♦ Q J x x   ♣ Q 10 x x

is worth 13 points for a takeout double of one heart—10 points in high cards and 3 points for the singleton heart.

♠ A K x x   ♥ x x   ♦ Q J x x   ♣ Q 10 x

is worth 13 points—12 points in high cards and 1 point for the doubleton heart.

♠ K J x x   ♥ none   ♦ A 10 x x x   ♣ 10 x x x

is worth 13 points—8 points in high cards and five points for the heart void.

♠ A K x   ♥ x x x   ♦ A x x x   ♣ K x x

is worth 13 points—14 points in high cards, less 1 point subtracted for holding only three spades. Remember, when you double one heart (or one club or one diamond) you count your support for spades. When you double one spade, you count your support for hearts.

We have deliberately picked examples which count to 13 points, since this is the minimum requirement for the double of a major suit. The double of a minor suit forces partner to bid at the one-level, not the two-level, so you may have as little as 11 points, valuing your hand in support of spades. For example, this would be an acceptable double of one club:

♠ A x x   ♥ K x x x   ♦ Q 10 x x x   ♣ x

You have 9 points in high cards plus 3 points for the singleton in the opponent's suit, less 1 point for only three spades —11 points in all.

These minimum standards for the takeout double—13 points over a major, 11 points over a minor—are only rough approximations. There are many, many factors which can affect your decision to enter the auction: if you are vulnerable and the opponents are not, you need a great deal more in high cards to double; if you have a lot of tens and nines or a wealth of Quick Tricks you need less; if much of your point-count is in the enemy suit you should be reluctant to double; if your opponents are timid, it pays to contest the auction a little more freely. But never lose sight of the guiding principle: *the nearer you come to the ideal three-suited pattern, the less you need in high cards.*

After Both Opponents Have Bid

When you are in fourth seat and both opponents have bid, the meaning of and requirements for a takeout double may alter. Three types of auction are possible. First, the enemy suit may have been raised (1 ♠—Pass—2 ♠—Double). Here your action has the same meaning as an immediate double of the opening one-bid. However, since you are forcing partner to bid at a higher level, you now need 15 points to double a major suit, 13 points to double a minor suit.

Second, there may have been a 1 NT response (1 ♡—Pass—1 NT—Double). In this case the double is still a takeout double of the opening suit (hearts, here) and promises support for the three unbid suits. Partner is forced to bid at the two-level, so you must have 13 points or more whether the opening was in a major or in a minor suit.

Third, your opponents may have bid two suits (1 ◊—Pass—1 ♠—Double). Now the double promises support for the two unbid suits (hearts and clubs in this instance), not for three suits. You may have an unbalanced two-suited hand like:

    ♠ xx   ♡ AQxxx   ◊ x   ♣ Kxxxx

or a relatively balanced hand like:

    ♠ xx   ♡ AQ10x   ◊ xxx   ♣ KQJx

By doubling, you promise 13 points in support of the unbid major, and length in the other unbid suit.

Responding to Partner's Double

When your partner has made a takeout double, most of the responsibility for getting to game is yours If you make a minimum, forced response the doubler will generally pass. Very seldom will he have a hand strong enough to make a safe rebid, since for all he knows you have a completely worthless hand and, by bidding again, he may be putting his neck on the chopping block. If you have the values to produce a game opposite a moderately strong takeout double, you must tell partner so with your first response.

The simplest try for game is to bid one more in your suit than you are forced to—to make a jump response (1 ♣ —Double—Pass—2 ♦; or 1 ♠—Double—Pass—3 ♡). These jumps are not forcing bids; they are not even very strong bids. They simply say, "Partner, I am not bidding entirely because you have forced me to—I have some useful cards." You do not need a long, strong suit in order to jump, for partner has promised you length in all unbid suits with his double. You are actually "supporting" doubler's suit when you respond.

Consequently, you value your cards as a supporting hand. Count your high-card points, and then add, for distribution, 1 point for each card over four in your trump suit and 1 point for each doubleton, 3 points for each singleton, 5 points for a void in a side suit. (You should tend to discount shortness in the opponent's suit, for partner is also short there, and this is duplicated value.) A total of 9 to 11 points is sufficient for a jump in a major suit, while to suggest an eleven-trick minor suit game you should have 11 to 13 points.

To illustrate, suppose your left-hand opponent opens one heart, partner doubles, your right hand opponent passes, and you hold:

♠ A J 10 x x   ♡ x x x   ♦ Q x x   ♣ x x

Jump to 2 ♠. You have 7 points in high cards, plus 1 point for the fifth spade and 1 point for the doubleton club, or 9 points in all. This hand does not look very strong, but remember that you would have been forced to respond *one* spade with only

♠ J x x x   ♡ x x x   ♦ x x x   ♣ x x x

If, on the same auction, you hold:

♠ K x   ♡ x x   ♦ K J 10 x x   ♣ Q x x x

Jump to 3 ♦. You have 11 points—9 in high cards, 1 for the fifth diamond, 1 for the doubleton spade (the doubleton heart does not count, for partner is also short in hearts.)

♠ K J x x   ♡ x x x   ◇ K 10 x x x   ♣ x

Jump to 2 ♠. You do not need a five-card suit to jump, for partner promises at least three spades with his double, and probably has four. Remember you are really supporting *his* suit. Always bid a major suit in preference to a minor suit in response to a takeout double. Major suits are the royal road to game.

When you are not strong enough for a positive (jump) response, you make a minimum response in a suit. Here, too, it is a good idea to bid a major suit if you have one, ahead of a minor suit. For example, if partner doubles 1 ♣ and you hold:

♠ J 10 x x   ♡ x x   ◇ K J x x x   ♣ x x

Bid 1 ♠, not 1 ◇. Your only real chance for game is to find partner with a very strong double and a fit for spades. But do not be afraid to respond in a minor suit, even at the two-level if you have no four-card major. Partner, with his double, promises support for all unbid suits.

What do you do with hands which are too strong for a jump response—hands which count to 12 points or more in support of a major suit or 14 points or more in support of a minor? You can jump directly to game, or you can cue-bid the opponent's suit (1 ♡—Double—Pass—2 ♡). This cue bid has nothing whatever to do with your holding in the enemy suit: if you wish to show first round control of their suit you must repeat the cue bid later. The bid says, "Partner, I'm pretty sure we have a game even if you have only a fair double, but I'm not quite sure what the contract should be."

Suppose partner doubles an enemy one-heart opening bid and you hold:

♠ K J x x   ♡ x x x   ◇ A K 10 x x   ♣ x

Here, you must bid 2 ♡. You are too strong merely to jump to three diamonds or two spades. As we saw earlier, you would bid two spades without the diamond ace. With this hand you must do more than suggest a game, but you cannot bid a game directly since you are not sure whether to play spades or diamonds.

Should partner make the expected two-spades response to your cue bid of two hearts, you will jump to four spades.

However, if he responds three clubs, you will rebid three diamonds to look for the minor-suit game.

Even after cue-bidding the opponent's suit, it is possible to give doubler a chance to quit under game. If you merely single-raise the suit doubler bids in response to your cue bid:

| 1 ♡ | Double | Pass | 2 ♡ |
| Pass | 2 ♠ | Pass | 3 ♠ |

you urge him strongly to go to game, but you do not force him to bid with a bare minimum. For example, the partnership hands might be

♠ K J x x	♠ A Q x x
♡ x x	♡ x x
◇ Q x x	◇ K J x x
♣ K J 10 x	♣ Q x x

OPPONENT	DOUBLER	OPPONENT	RESPONDER
1 ♡	Double	Pass	2 ♡
Pass	2 ♠	Pass	3 ♠
Pass	Pass	Pass	

Responder, with 12 points, is a little too strong to jump, and so cue-bids. However, since he has a minimum, he raises the two-spade rebid to three spades, not four spades. Doubler has a filthy hand—a bare, featureless 11 points counting the doubleton heart; therefore he is happy to quit. But if he held as little extra as the club ace in place of the king, he would go on to four spades.

Note that you have a continuous range of responses to a takeout double. On the auction: one heart—Double—?, with

Points	Hand
7 (0 to 8)	♠ K J x x ♡ x x x ◇ 10 x x x x ♣ x
	Bid: 1 ♠
10 (9-11)	♠ K J x x ♡ x x x ◇ K 10 x x x ♣ x
	Bid: 2 ♠
12 (12-13)	♠ K J x x ♡ x x x ◇ K Q x x x ♣ x
	Bid: 2 ♡, raise 2 ♠ to 3 ♠
14 (14-up)	♠ K J x x ♡ x x x ◇ A K x x x ♣ x
	Bid: 2 ♡, raise 2 ♠ to 4 ♠

Other strong bids are available after partner's takeout double. One of them is the response of 1 NT. (1 ♡—Double—Pass—1 NT). This is a constructive, strength-showing response, not a negative, weak one: if you have a poor hand, you must bid a suit. Partner's double may be based primarily on distributional values that will provide tricks only in a suit contract; 1 NT is probably the last response he wants to hear. So you must have 9 to 11 points in high cards plus solid stoppers in the opponent's suit before you make the bid. If partner doubles an enemy one-spade opening and you hold:

♠ Q 10 x x   ♡ x x x   ◇ x x x   ♣ x x x

Bid 2 ♣, not 1 NT. This is a nasty problem, but 1 NT is the worst possible answer to it. One notrump is the easiest contract for the opponents to double, and even if you get past the opponents you still have to reckon with partner, who, encouraged by your bid, may look for game. However, on the same auction with

♠ A Q x x   ♡ x x   ◇ K x x   ♣ J 10 x x

Bid 1 NT, not 2 ♣. Now you are safe in 1 NT even if partner has a distributional double, and if he has a respectable high-card holding you may well have a game at notrump.

Another strong action is to pass partner's takeout double for penalties. This should almost never be done, for the doubler may be completely unprepared for it. The "perfect" pattern for a takeout double—5-4-4 and void in the opponent's suit—is a horrible pattern for defense. In a sense, you are betraying partnership confidence when you pass a double, for partner, with

♠ K J x x   ♡ none   ◇ Q 10 x x x   ♣ K x x x

for example, should double a one-heart opening bid, but cannot afford to do so if you are going to leave the double in, even with

♠ Q x x   ♡ K J 9 x x   ◇ A x x   ♣ x x

With this hand you must respond 1 NT. Only if you are *solid* in the opponent's suit should you consider passing the double. Obviously, with

♠ Q x x   ♡ K Q J 9 x x   ◇ x x   ♣ A x

you will pass a takeout double of one heart for penalties. But if it is not this obvious that you must pass, bid.

Doubler's Rebid

Once you have made a takeout double, your subsequent action is largely a matter of arithmetic. When you have found a major-suit fit, 25 points between your hand and partner's will produce a sound play for game. Doubler's rebids are determined by this magic number, 25. Suppose you have doubled a one-heart opening bid with:

♠ AKxx   ♡ xx   ◊ KQxx   ♣ QJx

and partner responds one spade. What should you do?

Well, you have 16 points (15 points in high cards, 1 point for the doubleton) and partner has a maximum of 8 points, for with 9 points or more he would have jumped. So you must pass. Game is not in sight, for the most the combined hands can total is 24 points; when partner has a worthless hand even *two* spades may be in terrible jeopardy. But if, on the same auction, you hold:

♠ AKxx   ♡ x   ◊ KQxx   ♣ QJxx

you raise one spade to two spades. Now you have 18 points (counting 3 points for the singleton) and, by raising, you tell partner to bid for game if he has a maximum one-spade response—7 or 8 points in support. With

♠ AKxx   ♡ x   ◊ KQxx   ♣ AJxx

raise one spade to three spades. You have 20 points and, by jumping, ask partner to bid game with 5 or 6 points in support.

Adding to 25 is still the key when partner makes a jump response. He shows 9 to 11 points, so now you need 14 points to try for game and 16 points to be sure of game. Suppose you double a one-club opening bid and partner jumps to two hearts. With

13 points—♠ QJxx   ♡ AKxx   ◊ Qxx   ♣ xx—
Pass

15 points—♠ QJxx   ♡ AKxx   ◊ Axx   ♣ xx—
Bid 3 ♡

17 points—♠ QJxx   ♡ AKxx   ◊ Axxx   ♣ x—
Bid 4 ♡

Note that in each example in which you have raised partner's response you have held four trumps. This is mandatory even if the response was a jump; you cannot raise with only three trumps. Then, what if you have doubled one heart with

♠ Q J x   ♡ x   ◊ A J x x   ♣ A K J x x

and partner responds one spade? You have 18 points in support of spades (16 points in high cards plus 3 points for the singleton less 1 point for only three spades) and therefore game is a possibility; you must bid.

Bid two clubs, not two spades. This does not deny spade support, for when you doubled you promised at least three spades. The two-club bid announces a strong hand with three-card support. When doubler bids a new suit over partner's response, he is not "running out" of partner's suit; he is showing a powerful hand. Here is a typical sequence:

♠ Q x x   ♠ J 10 x x x
♡ A Q 10 x x   ♡ K x
◊ A J x x   ◊ K Q x
♣ x   ♣ x x x

OPPONENT	DOUBLER	OPPONENT	PARTNER
1 ♣	Double	Pass	2 ♠
Pass	3 ♡	Pass	4 ♠

The double and two-spade response are automatic. Doubler has 15 points in support of spades and so wants to invite game after responder's jump. He does this by bidding three hearts, not by raising spades, because he has only three trumps. Responder has an 11-point maximum jump (9 points in high cards, 1 point for the fifth spade, 1 point for the doubleton heart) and so leaps to game over three hearts. He is not worried about the trump suit—doubler promised three spades with his first call. If doubler's hand were

♠ Q x   ♡ A Q J x x x   ◊ A J x x   ♣ x

he would not have doubled one club, but would have overcalled with one heart instead.

THE OVERCALL

The overcall, unlike the double, has no specific distributional pattern to distinguish it. Whenever you wish to enter the auction, but find your distribution unsuitable for a takeout double, you overcall. Of course, many hands are too weak for an overcall, and one hand in a thousand is too strong. In deciding whether to overcall, you must consider both strength and distribution.

When is your distribution unsuitable for a takeout double? Primarily, when you are short in one unbid suit. Suppose, in each of these next examples, that an opponent opens the bidding with one club. If you are next to speak, with:

♠ xx   ♡ AKJxx   ◇ AQxxx   ♣ x

Overcall 1 ♡. Never double with a two-suited hand—first, because the double promises support which you cannot deliver for the third suit; second, because you want to bid both your suits, and the double robs you of one opportunity. Even with a two-suiter in spades and hearts, you should overcall, not double.

♠ KQ   ♡ AQxxx   ◇ Axx   ♣ xxx

Overcall 1 ♡. A doubleton spade, even though a strong doubleton, makes the takeout double impossible. You cannot afford to force a spade bid from partner, although you can support the suit if he bids it voluntarily.

♠ Q10x   ♡ AKJxx   ◇ x   ♣ Kxxx

Overcall 1 ♡. This would be a reasonable double if the opening bid were one diamond, but you cannot double one club with a singleton diamond. To double and then bid hearts over partner's diamond response would show great strength, not distaste for partner's suit.

Even if you have length in all unbid suits, your hand may be unsuitable for a double. When you have a strong suit of your own that is likely to prove a better trump suit than one which partner has been forced to name, you should overcall, not double. For example, over a one-diamond opening, with:

♠ AKJxx   ♡ xxx   ◇ x   ♣ KQxx

Overcall 1 ♠. You have every reason to believe that spades is the suit to play in. If partner bids hearts or clubs voluntarily you will be happy to raise him. But you want partner to be in a position to raise you if he has three spades and a fairly good hand. On the same auction, with:

♠ Q x x   ♡ A K J x x x   ◇ x   ♣ K x x

Overcall 1 ♡. You can support all unbid suits, but since you have a strong preference for play in hearts you should overcall, not double. You are not strong enough to double and then bid two hearts over a one-spade or two-club response. This would show about 19 points in support of partner's suit, instead of which you have only 15 points.

How much strength is needed for an overcall? You will have noticed that all the examples of overcalls given thus far have been the equivalent of sound opening bids. Then is the requirement 12 or 14 or 16 points? No, for the factors involved cannot be measured in points. The answer is to overcall when the possible gain outweighs the fearful risk.

For never forget that the overcall is the most dangerous bid in bridge. When you bid two clubs over an enemy one-spade opening, you contract to win 8 out of 13 tricks—this in face of the fact that you know nothing about partner's hand, while you do know that at least one opponent is strong. And when your overcall is doubled by your left-hand opponent you desperately need a few useful cards in partner's hand; but just then is when he is likely to have a Yarborough, for there are almost no high cards left for him to hold. It is no wonder that the juiciest sets come from penalty doubles of overcalls.

Nor is an immediate double of your overcall the only danger. Partner, encouraged by your bid, may take action of his own which will place you in jeopardy. This is particularly true as *we* play, for our overcalls do not limit the strength of our hands. Thus, partner must keep the auction alive with very little.

So grave are these risks that one modern bidding school has virtually abandoned direct overcalls. They stay out of the early rounds of bidding. If the opponents stop at a low contract, they then enter the auction, confident that partner must have some cards, otherwise the enemy would have gone further. Now, this is not a completely foolish policy. With a hand like

♠ x x x   ♡ x x   ◇ A x x   ♣ A Q J x x

it is very, very dangerous to overcall two clubs when an opponent opens one spade. But, strangely enough, it is relatively safe to bid *three* clubs on the auction:

1 ♠	Pass	2 ♠	Pass
Pass	3 ♣		

The opponents have found a fit, so you and partner probably have a fit also. Despite their fit, the enemy stopped at a low level, so partner is sure to hold some valuable high cards. These reopening bids are called "balancing" and will be discussed fully in the next chapter.

The principal flaw in waiting to "balance" with almost all hands, instead of bidding directly with some, is that you will miss games. Partner will rarely move toward game over your balancing bid—he will presume, even if he has quite a fair hand, that you knew from the opponent's auction that he had strength, that you were bidding his cards as well as your own. If a smattering of high cards or a long suit in partner's hand will produce a game, you must bid directly to tell him so.

Therefore, in deciding whether you are strong enough to overcall you must ask yourself three questions:

1. *If my overcall is doubled, how much can I be hurt?*
2. *If partner bids over my overcall, will my hand support a higher contract?*
3. *What are our chances for game?*

The answer to Question 1 lies mainly in the solidity of your trump suit. If you overcall two clubs with:

    ♠ J x   ♡ Q x   ◇ A 10 x   ♣ K Q x x x x

and are doubled, you may be set as many as four or five tricks. Or, just as bad, you may be set two or three tricks when the opponents could make no more than a partial on their own. But if your two-club overcall is made with:

    ♠ x x   ♡ x x   ◇ A Q x   ♣ K Q J 10 x x

you will not be set more than one or two tricks. And if you do go down, the opponents will have beaten you through an abundance of high cards and surely could have made a game themselves. If you are certain to take a lot of trump tricks, the enemy will never get rich doubling you.

Obviously, the level at which you bid is important too. An overcall at the one level is less dangerous than an overcall at the two level and much less risky than one at the three level.

Vulnerability is another factor. When you are vulnerable, the increased scale of penalties means that you need an extra margin of safety.

In general, you should try to stay within 500 points of your bid. If your overcall is doubled and partner has a normally distributed bad hand, you should expect to be set no more than 500 points.

Questions 2 and 3 (Will your hand support a higher contract if partner bids? What are your chances for game?) are related, and their answer lies in high-card structure, in Quick Tricks. Consider these two hands:

a. ♠ xx　♡ xx　◇ QJ10　♣ KQJ10xx
b. ♠ xx　♡ Ax　◇ AJx　♣ AJxxxx

Suppose your opponent opens one spade. With which hand should you overcall two clubs? Both hands figure to win about 6 tricks on their own, but Hand "b" might take fewer if the trump suit splits badly. Hand "a," then, is a safer overcall than "b." Yet you should overcall with "b" and not with "a."

Hand "a" is good for nothing except play in two clubs. To make a game, partner would need a strong enough hand to overcall or double independently. But Hand "b" will produce game facing many hands with which partner himself cannot enter the bidding. Suppose partner has

♠ xx　♡ KQxxxx　◇ Kxx　♣ xx

and the auction goes:

OPPONENT	YOU	OPPONENT	PARTNER
1 ♠	2 ♣	2 ♠	3 ♡

If you have Hand "b" for your two-club overcall, you will bid four hearts and probably score a game. But if you have "a" you are already in serious trouble and will be lucky to escape a severe penalty. Suppose partner has:

♠ Kx　♡ Kxxx　◇ Kxxxxx　♣ x

and bids

OPPONENT	YOU	OPPONENT	PARTNER
1 ♠	2 ♣	2 ♠	3 ◇

If you have Hand "a," three diamonds is down one or two tricks even though you have a diamond fit, but if you hold Hand "b" you will make game (and possibly slam) at diamonds. Suppose partner has

♠ AQx ♡ QJxx ◇ Kxx ♣ xxx

and bids

OPPONENT	YOU	OPPONENT	PARTNER
1 ♠	2 ♣	2 ♠	3 NT

With Hand "b" you are a favorite to make game, but with Hand "a" you are just waiting for the axe to fall.

Note that the hand with the wealth of Quick Tricks is useful in many different contracts (and on defense, too, should partner double an enemy contract). It is worthwhile to incur a little extra risk overcalling with such a hand because the chance for gain is so great.

This is the type of decision you must make each time you overcall. You must weigh the extent of *risk* in bidding —the danger of an immediate double, the danger that partner will get you overboard—against the likelihood of *gain* from bidding—the chance that you can score a game. Hands with 3½ Quick Tricks or more present such strong game prospects that you should overcall in almost any long suit, without worrying about its solidity. As your high card structure decreases from 3½ to 2½ Quick Tricks, you require increasingly longer and stronger suits. And with fewer than 2 Quick Tricks you should almost never overcall.

Here are a few examples. In each case, the opponent has opened one heart and you are next to speak.

♠ xx ♡ xx ◇ AKxx ♣ AQxxx

Bid 2 ♣. Your suit is weak, but with so much top card strength you must act immediately.

♠ xx ♡ Qx ◇ Axxx ♣ AQxxx

Pass. Now there is little danger of missing game by passing, so the danger of being doubled is decisive.

♠ AQxxx ♡ xx ◇ Axxx ♣ Qx

Bid 1 ♠. This is the same hand as above but with spades instead of clubs. The difference is that when your suit is a major there is more prospect of game, so your likelihood of gain is increased. And your overcall is at the one-level, so the extent of risk is less.

Responding to Overcalls

When partner overcalls, just as when he opens the bidding, you should make some bid if your hand contains a useful feature. Since partner may have a very strong hand for his overcall, you must make a determined effort to keep the auction alive for him.

The weakest action available is the single raise. By raising, you announce 6 to 9 points in support of partner's suit, counting distribution. Clearly, with so little strength you can have no great desire to reach a high contract; you are merely giving partner another chance to bid in case he needs very little help to make game. And even when partner's overcall is a minimum, your raise is useful, for it serves to crowd the bidding for the opponents. Look at this deal, taken from a team-of-four match we played last year.

West dealer
Both sides vulnerable

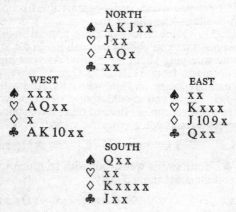

NORTH
♠ A K J x x
♡ J x x
◇ A Q x
♣ x x

WEST
♠ x x x
♡ A Q x x
◇ x
♣ A K 10 x x

EAST
♠ x x
♡ K x x x
◇ J 10 9 x
♣ Q x x

SOUTH
♠ Q x x
♡ x x
◇ K x x x x
♣ J x x

When our teammates were East and West and our opponents North and South, the auction went

WEST	NORTH	EAST	SOUTH
1 ♣	Double	Pass	1 ◇
1 ♡	1 ♠	2 ♡	2 ♠
4 ♡	Pass	Pass	Pass

The vulnerable game contract was easily fulfilled. When the hand was replayed at our table, we held the North-

South cards and our opponents were East and West. Our auction:

WEST	NORTH	EAST	SOUTH
1 ♣	1 ♠	Pass	2 ♠
Pass	Pass	Pass	

Having a distinct preference for play in spades, we overcall, rather than double, with the North cards. This enables South to make his light raise to two spades. Notice that West would now be obliged to bid the heart suit at the three-level instead of at the one-level, and he is too weak to do so. As a result, we "stole" the contract and made two spades our way!

Observe that North passed South's raise. Just as if he had opened the bidding one spade and had been raised to two spades, North needed a better bid from partner to envision game. With a stronger hand, South could have jumped to three spades or could have bid a new suit.

The jump raise of an overcall is not a forcing bid. It announces 10 to 12 points in support, and invites the overcaller to proceed to game unless he has a bare minimum. If, in the previous example, South held the club ace additional

 ♠ Qxx ♡ xx ◇ Kxxxx ♣ Axx

he would raise partner's one-spade overcall to *three* spades. He has 10 points in support—9 in high cards plus 1 for the doubleton heart.

The takeout to a new suit (1 ♣—1 ♠—Pass—2 ◇) is used when the partner of the overcaller wishes to move towards game, but is uncertain about which game to reach. This is a strong, forcing bid. Partner is not "running out" of overcaller's suit—he is trying for game. For example on the auction:

OPPONENT	PARTNER	OPPONENT	YOU
1 ♡	2 ◇	Pass	?

 ♠ AKJxxx ♡ xx ◇ Qx ♣ xxx

Bid 2 ♠. Overcaller must not pass the change of suit—if he rebids 2 NT you will raise to 3 NT; if he rebids three spades you will go on to four spades; if he rebids three diamonds you will invite with four diamonds. But on the same auction, with:

♠ Q 10 x x x ♥ x x x ♦ Q x ♣ x x x

Pass. Two diamonds is a perfectly satisfactory contract. Do not disturb it. And with:

♠ Q J 10 x x x x ♥ x x ♦ x x ♣ x x

Bid 3 ♠. The jump shift is pre-emptive after an over-call. You use it with a long suit and a worthless hand. Your object is not to get to game but to impede the enemy.

If you are strong enough to insist on going to game once partner overcalls, you can cue-bid the opponent's suit (1 ♥—1 ♠—Pass—2 ♥). This is an artificial bid which forces partner to keep the auction alive until game is reached; it says nothing about your holding in the suit bid. Normally, you would use the cue bid if you wanted room to investigate slam or to choose among several possible game contracts. For example you should bid two hearts (1 ♥—1 ♠—Pass—2 ♥) with:

♠ A x ♥ x x x ♦ K Q x x ♣ A Q x x

You know there is a game, but you do not know where. But when you do know where you want to play the hand, jump directly to game. (1 ♥—1 ♠—Pass—4 ♠; 1♠— 2 ♦—Pass—3 NT) rather than prolong the auction with cue-bids or other forces, which can only help the opponents.

PRE-EMPTIVE JUMP OVERCALLS

Earlier in this chapter, we said that you should not bid 2 ♣ over an enemy 1 ♠ opening if you hold

♠ x x ♥ x x ♦ Q J 10 ♣ K Q J 10 x x

Does it disturb you to pass? It should. True, this hand offers little prospect of game, but by entering the auction you may reach a profitable sacrifice, get partner off to a winning opening lead, or, most important, interrupt your opponents' communications. Therefore, we do not pass with this type of hand. Instead of overcalling two clubs, we use the jump overcall to *three* clubs.

The jump overcall is a weak, pre-emptive bid. It puts

partner on notice right away that we are not looking for game, so we no longer have to worry that he will get us into trouble. And the jump overcall makes it easier for partner to sacrifice against an enemy game contract, assuring him that we do not have great defensive strength. Most important, the pre-emptive jump does a really effective job of disrupting the opponents' auction. A two-club bid over one spade takes away little bidding room, but a *three*-club bid robs the enemy of one full level, and a crucial level at that.

Here again we jump with the weaker hand to crowd the bidding for the opponents, and go slow with the stronger hand, to leave ourselves room for investigation. As always, there is risk in this, especially when our suit is not so solid as in the example. But in bridge there is rarely gain without risk. It is relatively safe to overcall one spade with:

♠ A J 9 x x x   ♥ x x   ♦ J x x   ♣ x x

when your opponent opens one heart. But it is so futile.

In contrast, if you jump to *two* spades over one heart you are taking an appreciably greater risk. But now you can accomplish something with your bid. Here is the complete deal from a recent tournament.

South dealer
North-South vulnerable

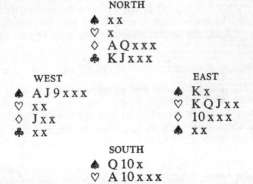

NORTH
♠ x x
♥ x
♦ A Q x x x
♣ K J x x x

WEST
♠ A J 9 x x x
♥ x x
♦ J x x
♣ x x

EAST
♠ K x
♥ K Q J x x
♦ 10 x x x
♠ x x

SOUTH
♠ Q 10 x
♥ A 10 x x x
♦ K
♣ A Q x x

The most common auction was:

SOUTH	WEST	NORTH	EAST
1 ♡	1 ♠	2 ◇	Pass
2 NT	Pass	3 ♣	Pass
5 ♣	Pass	Pass	Pass

The five-club contract is easily fulfilled. At our table, the auction was:

SOUTH	WEST	NORTH	EAST
1 ♡	2 ♠	3 ◇	Pass
3 NT	Pass	Pass	Pass

and 3 NT was defeated two tricks, a difference of 800 points. This was quite a handsome return for the extra risk the jump entailed. Our opponents desperately needed the round of bidding that we stole from them with the pre-emptive jump overcall.

Overcall or Jump Overcall?

How do you determine which to make—an overcall or a jump overcall? Basically, it is a question of why you are bidding. If you want to bid because there is a genuine prospect that the hand "belongs" to your side, possibly for a game, then make the simple overcall. But if you want to bid in order to crowd the opponent's auction or to find a sacrifice, then jump. It is up to your individual judgment which bid to use—there are no hard and fast rules. Many hands, in fact, are susceptible to both treatments. Suppose you hold

♠ x x ♡ x x ◇ K Q J 10 x x ♣ A x x

If you are in second seat and an opponent, first hand, opens one heart, it is probably best to bid two diamonds. This is a very skinny overcall, but you have two Quick Tricks with a solid suit, and there is a real chance that partner may have enough controls in the side suits to produce 3 NT.

But if you are in fourth seat and after two passes your opponent, third hand, opens one heart, the situation has changed. Partner now is a passed hand, and it is much less likely that he can produce the stoppers and tricks needed to make 3 NT. With your prospects for game diminished, you would be better advised to bid *three* diamonds to take advantage of the pre-emptive value of the jump.

In general, you can guide yourself by Quick Tricks. With 2½ Quick Tricks or more, you should almost never use the pre-emptive jump. It is hands with 1½ Quick Tricks or fewer that are ideal jump overcalls if they have considerable playing strength. As with all pre-emptive bids, the pattern to look for is offensive, not defensive strength.

An error to guard against is using the simple overcall because you are too weak to jump. When your opponent opens one heart and you are next to bid with

♠ K J x x x x   ♡ x x   ◇ x   ♣ Q 10 x x

you may bid two spades if you wish. But if you are vulnerable and fear that the set will be too great if two spades is doubled, pass; do *not* bid *one* spade. To overcall, you should be *too strong* for the pre-emptive jump, not too weak.

Responding to the Pre-emptive Jump Overcall

When partner has made a pre-emptive jump overcall, you must remember, above all else, that he does not want to hear from you. He is not describing his hand to you, asking you to take action based on his bid. His bid is tactical, not descriptive; his primary aim is to prevent the enemy from proceeding to their best contract at their own leisurely pace. To take away the opponents' bidding room, he is deliberately overbidding, gambling against a double.

Partner has won his gamble when the next opponent does not double him. Unless you have absolutely clear-cut action to take, pass and be content with whatever advantage partner's bid gives your side. Suppose, on the auction

OPPONENT	PARTNER	OPPONENT	YOU
1 ◇	2 ♠	3 ♡	?

you hold: ♠ K x x   ♡ x x   ◇ x x x x   ♣ A 10 x x

Pass! Do not get the idea that, because you have a fit for partner's suit, you must bid something. Partner's jump has distorted the opponents' auction—be satisfied with that. The complete deal may be:

```
                        NORTH
                    ♠ x x
                    ♡ A K Q x x
                    ◇ J x x
                    ♣ Q x x
        WEST                            EAST
    ♠ Q J 10 x x x                  ♠ K x x
    ♡ 10 x x x                      ♡ x x
    ◇ A                             ◇ x x x x
    ♣ x x                           ♣ A 10 x x
                        SOUTH
                    ♠ A x
                    ♡ J x
                    ◇ K Q 10 x x
                    ♣ K J x x
```

Notice that if you (East) pass throughout, the auction is likely to go:

SOUTH	WEST	NORTH	EAST
1 ◇	2 ♠	3 ♡	Pass
3 NT	Pass	Pass	Pass

South is forced to bid over three hearts, and he bids 3 NT mostly for lack of anything better to do. But North will probably accept the contract, for he has no way of knowing that South is not eager to play at notrump. Thus, the enemy may be crowded into a terrible contract which you will defeat three tricks.

Now see what happens if East shows his spade support:

SOUTH	WEST	NORTH	EAST
1 ◇	2 ♠	3 ♡	3 ♠
Pass	Pass	4 ◇	Pass
4 ♡ (?)	Pass	Pass	Pass

South is no longer forced to bid, and is grateful for the opportunity to pass. North-South are out of the woods—they will play either in four diamonds or four hearts and make the contract. East's pointless three-spade bid took the pressure off the enemy and dissipated all the advantage gained by West's jump.

When, then, should you bid after partner's jump over-call? Normally, only when you intend to sacrifice against an enemy game contract. And then you should take your sacrifice *immediately,* giving the opponents as little room as possible. For example, on the auction

OPPONENT	PARTNER	OPPONENT	YOU
1 ♣	2 ♠	Pass	?

♠ Q 10 x x   ♡ x x x   ◇ A 10 x x x   ♣ x

Jump to four spades. The opponents are cold for a game, but they don't know it yet. Prevent them from finding out.

On the auction:

OPPONENT	PARTNER	OPPONENT	YOU
1 ◇	2 ♡	2 ♠	?

holding   ♠ A x   ♡ K Q x x   ◇ J x x x x x   ♣ x
do not make the error of bidding three hearts or even four hearts. You intend to sacrifice over an enemy four spade contract, so jump to five hearts right away. The opening bidder has not yet had an opportunity to support spades, so perhaps he may be stampeded into an unmakeable five spade or six spade contract.

Now these are very brave bids that we have just described, for they contract to take 10 or 11 tricks with a poor hand facing another poor hand. We are not recommending that you do this often—it requires four-card or better support, some shortness in a side suit, a little, but not too much defensive strength. The central point that we want to make is that unless you have the perfect hand to justify violent action, you should allow partner's preemptive jump overcall to bar you from the auction.

OTHER DEFENSIVE BIDS

The Cue Bid

At the start of our discussion of overcalls, we mentioned that once in a thousand deals you will have a hand too strong for an overcall. Suppose an opponent opens one heart and you hold

♠ A K Q 10 x x x   ♡ x   ◇ A Q x x   ♣ A

Obviously, you are unwilling to bid only one spade, since partner may well pass and you have game in your own hand. However, to bid four spades would be to give up all chance of reaching slam. So you bid two hearts, the direct cue bid of the opponent's suit, forcing partner to respond and telling him that you have a powerhouse.

You may also use the cue bid when you have the pattern for a takeout double. Over a one-diamond opening bid, with:

♠ AKJx   ♡ AKQx   ◇ x   ♣ KQ10x

it is probably best to bid two diamonds, to indicate the unusual strength of your hand.

It is seldom wise to cue-bid with a two-suited hand, however strong, for your first duty is to bid both your suits. If you cue-bid two clubs over one club with:

♠ x   ♡ AKQ10xx   ◇ AKJxx   ♣ x

you may find that the opponents have pre-empted the auction up to the five-level before you get a chance to bid either hearts or diamonds. The risk of overcalling one heart—that you will be passed out there—is not great at all. When you have such a freak, someone else at the table will find a bid.

The 1 NT Overcall

Another rare defensive bid is the overcall of 1 NT. No bid is more dangerous than this, for the normal jeopardy of an overcall is heightened here by the ease with which the enemy can double 1 NT. Your left-hand opponent does not need strength in any particular suit in order to double you. Since he knows that his partner has an opening bid, he can double 1 NT on a smattering of high cards. Whenever you are in trouble you are sure to be doubled; and whenever you are doubled you are sure to be in trouble.

In consequence, we overcall 1 NT only when very strong. A point-count of 18, with at least two stoppers in the opponent's suit, is ideal. This can be shaded down to 17 points or up to 19 points. A typical overcall of 1 NT after an enemy one-spade opening would be:

♠ KJx   ♡ AQ   ◇ A10xx   ♣ KJxx

The Trap Pass

There is another reason for the rarity of the 1 NT overcall. When you have substantial strength in the opponent's suit, it will often pay you to pass even a powerful hand. This is the "trap" pass, made in the hope that the enemy can be subjected to a severe penalty later in the auction. Study this deal, for example:

South dealer
Both sides vulnerable

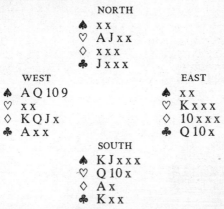

NORTH
♠ x x
♡ A J x x
♢ x x x
♣ J x x x

WEST
♠ A Q 10 9
♡ x x
♢ K Q J x
♣ A x x

EAST
♠ x x
♡ K x x x
♢ 10 x x x
♣ Q 10 x

SOUTH
♠ K J x x x
♡ Q 10 x
♢ A x
♣ K x x

South will open one spade, and West, in many systems, has the strength to overcall 1 NT. If he does, the auction will be:

SOUTH	WEST	NORTH	EAST
1 ♠	1 NT	Pass	Pass
Pass			

and the contract will be fulfilled with an overtrick, for a small profit. But if West trap-passes, the auction should go:

SOUTH	WEST	NORTH	EAST
1 ♠	Pass	1 NT	Pass
Pass	Double	Pass	Pass
Pass			

East should lead a spade (he knows that West has a powerful hand and passed at his first opportunity only because he had spade strength) and East-West will rack up an 800-point penalty.

Is it not dangerous to pass over an enemy opening bid when you have a strong hand? What if your left-hand opponent passes also? Nothing bad can happen. If your partner passes, ending the auction, neither side can make much. For if partner has the strong suit or the 9 to 10 points needed to make a game your way, he will keep the auction alive. This reopening position is covered in the next chapter under "Balancing."

Chapter 9

Balancing

By LISTENING to the opponent's auction, you can discover (within broad limits) how much strength they have, and, thus, how strong your partner's hand is. That is the underlying theory of "balancing bids." When your opponents stop bidding at a low level, you can sometimes tell with virtual certainty that partner has a strong hand even though he has never bid. Therefore, in certain specialized situations you can make bids which appear incredibly reckless, but which are actually safe and sound.

The most basic of these balancing positions occurs when your left-hand opponent opens the bidding with one of a suit, partner passes, and your right-hand opponent passes also. Your decision to reopen or to pass out an auction like

OPPONENT	PARTNER	OPPONENT	YOU
1 ♡	Pass	Pass	?

cannot be based on *your* thirteen cards alone; this brief auction has told you quite a lot about your partner's hand. For example, suppose the one-heart opening has been passed around to you and you hold:

♠ Kxxxxx   ♡ xx   ◇ xx   ♣ Q 10 x

This is a miserably weak hand and hardly seems worth a bid. But reflect—give your left-hand opponent a topnotch opening bid of 18 points; give your right-hand opponent 3 points for his pass; counting in your 5 points, all this adds up to only 26 points. So partner has at least 14 points; he has made a trap pass over one heart with a sound opening bid in high cards. If partner had opened the bidding, would you allow the enemy to buy the contract for one heart? And here you know not only that partner has an opening bid, but that his high cards are advantageously placed, for they are sitting behind the enemy's strength. The full deal may be:

NORTH
♠ A x
♡ A J x x x
♢ x x
♣ A J x x

WEST
♠ Q x
♡ K Q 10 x x
♢ A K J x
♣ K x

EAST
♠ J 10 x
♡ 9
♢ Q 10 9 x x
♣ 9 x x x

SOUTH
♠ K x x x x
♡ x x
♢ x x
♣ Q 10 x

North has no option but to pass over West's one-heart opening, for there is no bid he can properly make. Moreover, he has high hopes for a substantial penalty should East act. It is *South* who must bid if his side is to reach its partial score contract in spades.

Actually South must bid not only to compete for a partial, but for fear of missing a game! Even in the example above, North-South are very close to making four spades, although they do not have the strength to bid above the 2 or 3 level. But if West's opening is on 15 points instead of 18, if North has West's heart king or club king, a contract of four spades should be reached and made. And North will still pass over one heart with

♠ A x   ♡ A J x x x   ♢ x x   ♣ A K J x

for he has no satisfactory direct action to take. He relies on partner to balance, to protect his trap pass.

Then should you ever pass and end the auction? Indeed yes—there are two great groups of hands with which you will not balance.

With fewer than 8 points and no distributional feature, do not balance. If a one-heart opening bid is passed around to you and you hold

♠ Q x x   ♡ 10 x x   ♢ J x x x   ♣ K x x

Pass. It is still likely that your side can make a partial score, but the enemy will probably go down one or two tricks at one heart to compensate you for this. The point is that it is not possible that you have a game. With 18 points or more partner would have acted directly over one heart.

There is another group of hands with which you should not balance—those with length and strength in the opponent's suit. You may pass even a fairly strong hand in this position. On the same auction as before, you hold:

♠ K x   ♡ A Q 10 x x   ◇ K x x   ♣ x x x

Pass. Your partner is short in the enemy suit, yet he took no action over one heart, not even a pre-emptive jump overcall or a light takeout double. Probably he has 7 or 8 points without a long suit, and your side can make very little. You have an excellent hand for defense against hearts but a poor one for offense, as your strength is now badly placed—the heart honors are behind yours, whatever aces the enemy has are behind your kings. Strangely, it is in many respects preferable not to have too strong a hand in the reopening position! You need fewer points to make game when your side's high cards are concentrated behind the opening bidder.

How to Reopen

There are three ways to reopen the auction when the opening bid is passed around to you—you can double, overcall, or bid 1 NT. Your choice among them is dictated primarily by the strength of your hand.

"Double" is the strongest action. It says that you have a worthy hand of your own; that you are not merely "protecting" partner's possible trap pass. Normally you should have 11 points or more in high cards for the call, but 10 points might do in a pinch. There are no rigid distributional requirements for this reopening double, as there are for all other takeout doubles; your strength is the paramount consideration. After all, you will reopen the auction with 5-point hands and with 25-point hands. Clearly, your first concern must be to narrow this range as sharply as you can.

The reopening overcall (1 ♡—Pass—Pass—2 ◇) is a *weak* bid; it says that you have a long suit and are counting on partner's hand for the high cards needed to make your contract. You should have fewer than 11 points, for otherwise you would double. The jump overcall (1 ♡—

Pass—Pass—2 ♠) is not pre-emptive in the reopening position. It is made with a 10- to 12-point hand which has a long, good-looking suit. You are too strong for a simple overcall, strong enough to double; but you are too weak to double and then bid your suit over partner's response. (This sequence is reserved to describe a really powerful hand, as though you were doubling and then bidding again in the *immediate* position instead of the *reopening* position.)

The reopening bid of 1 NT (1 ♡ —Pass—Pass—1 NT) is *weak*. It says that you have 8 to 10 points with no long suit; again you are bidding partner's cards. If partner has "trapped" with 15 or 16 points you may well make 3 NT. Incidentally, you need not worry too much about having stoppers in the enemy suit for your bid—partner has cards in their suit; that is why he passed at his first opportunity.

Suppose one heart is opened on your left and passed around to you. You hold:

♠ A Q 10 x x   ♡ K x x   ◊ x x   ♣ Q J x

Double. It is more important to tell partner about your strength than to show your spade suit.

♠ A Q 10 x x   ♡ x x x   ◊ x x   ♣ Q x x

Bid 1 ♠. With 8 points you are too weak to double; you overcall.

♠ A Q J x x x   ♡ K J x   ◊ x x   ♣ x x

Bid 2 ♠. You are strong enough to double, but not to double and bid two spades over a two-club or two-diamond response. For this you would need at least another king.

♠ A Q x   ♡ J x x   ◊ x x x   ♣ Q x x x

Bid 1 NT. You must not pass, for your side may have a game. This bid looks dangerous, but nothing terrible will happen to you—your partner has a strong hand.

BALANCING LATER IN THE AUCTION

An opponent's opening bid passed around to you is the most common occasion for balancing, but by no means the only one. Even when *both* opponents bid you may wish to balance if they stop at a low contract. However, there is an important difference. The fact that the enemy are willing to end their auction at a low level does not in itself mean that they are weak in high cards. You cannot automatically count on partner for the "missing" strength.

For when the opponents stop bidding early there can be *two* explanations: 1) They have found a fit but are too weak to go further. 2) They have not found a fit and are therefore afraid to bid any more regardless of their strength. Clearly it can be very profitable to balance in the first instance—with very little risk, you may push the opponents beyond their depth or even find that the hand "belongs" to you. But just as clearly, it can be disastrous to balance in the second instance—you will probably sustain a crushing penalty. The knack of balancing lies in learning to distinguish between the two situations.

Suppose you are second hand and hold

♠ A J x x x　♡ x x　◇ Q J x x　♣ x x

The bidding is opened with one heart to your right; you pass; two hearts is bid on your left; partner passes; opening bidder passes. *You should balance with two spades.* This is clear-cut, since the opponents have found a fit and stopped short. When *they* have a fit, *you* have a fit too. When *they* do not have the high cards to try for game, *partner* has them. There are always 40 points in the deck. The full deal is probably much like:

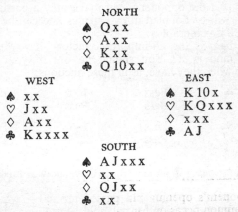

NORTH
♠ Q x x
♡ A x x
◇ K x x
♣ Q 10 x x

WEST
♠ x x
♡ J x x
◇ A x x
♣ K x x x x

EAST
♠ K 10 x
♡ K Q x x x
◇ x x x
♣ A J

SOUTH
♠ A J x x x
♡ x x
◇ Q J x x
♣ x x

Note that the enemy can make two hearts; you can make two spades.

Now suppose you hold the same hand with which you

balanced above and hear this auction: One-diamond opening on your right, one-heart response on your left; two-club bid on your right, two-heart rebid on your left; passed around to you.

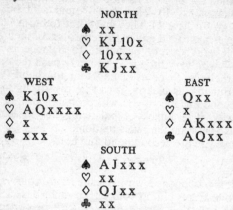

NORTH
♠ x x
♡ K J 10 x
♢ 10 x x
♣ K J x x

WEST
♠ K 10 x
♡ A Q x x x x
♢ x
♣ x x x

EAST
♠ Q x x
♡ x
♢ A K x x x
♣ A Q x x

SOUTH
♠ A J x x x
♡ x x
♢ Q J x x
♣ x x

Here it would be *suicidal* for you to balance with two spades. The opponents have not found a fit, so you may have none either. And the enemy stopped bidding because they had no fit, not because they were weak; so partner is not marked with much strength.

Note that the opponents can make only a partial score, but you will be doubled in two spades and can be set 900 (or 1400 if vulnerable).

Fit, then, is the all-important factor—have the opponents found a fit? You should go out of your way to balance when they have, as in these auctions:

| 1 ♣ | Pass | 1 ♢ | Pass |
| 2 ♢ | Pass | Pass | ? |

1 ♣	Pass	1 ♢	Pass
1 ♡	Pass	2 ♡	Pass
Pass	?		

You must never balance when they show a misfit, as in these:

1 ♣	Pass	1 ♡	Pass
2 ♣	Pass	2 ♡	Pass
Pass	?		

| 1 ♡ | Pass | 2 ◊ | Pass |
| 2 ♡ | Pass | Pass | ? |

There is still a third type of auction, in which the opponents clearly limit their strength, but do not indicate whether or not they have good fitting hands. For example,

| 1 ♠ | Pass | 1 NT | Pass |
| Pass | ? | | |

| 1 ♡ | Pass | 1 NT | Pass |
| 2 ♡ | Pass | Pass | ? |

Here there is no reason to believe that you will find a fit with partner, although you can count on him for substantial high card values, since neither opponent can be strong. You can balance, therefore, *but only when you have a long suit* and need strength, not fit, from partner.

When the opponents have found a fit and stopped at a low contract, how do you balance—with a double or an overcall? Earlier we gave an example of balancing when the opponents have bid 1 ♡—2 ♡ and passed. With

♠ A J x x x   ♡ x x   ◊ Q J x x   ♣ x x

you should overcall two spades, for you have a reasonably strong suit to bid and can count on partner for high cards. If, however, you held partner's hand in the example deal—

♠ Q x x   ♡ A x x   ◊ K x x   ♣ Q 10 x x

and he yours, you should balance with a double, counting on partner to have a suit. He, then, would bid two spades, and you would reach the same contract. Almost invariably, one partner will have the suit and the other will have the high cards in these true balancing positions. (Obviously, if one partner had both high cards and suit he would have bid directly instead of waiting to balance.) When the auction is passed around to the partner with the high cards, he balances with a double; when to the partner with the suit, he balances with an overcall. It is as simple as that.

On these auctions which call for balancing action only if you have a long suit

| 1 ♠ | Pass | 1 NT | Pass |
| Pass | ? | | |

for example, the reopening double has a different meaning; for with a smattering of high cards and no distributional feature you would pass. The double here is not a balancing bid at all, but means that you were trapping over one spade with a very strong hand, and are doubling 1 NT for penalties.

Never forget that when your partner makes a balancing overcall or double he is not looking for game; if he were, he would have acted directly. He is merely trying to prevent the enemy from buying a cheap contract, *so do not punish him for this* by getting him too high. In an earlier example, one player held:

♠ Q x x   ♡ A x x   ◇ K x x   ♣ Q 10 x x

and heard his partner balance with two spades after the opponents passed out in two hearts. He must not say to himself, "Here my partner is contracting to take eight tricks, and I have never shown him my spade fit or my 11 points. I had better raise him." He must realize that partner has already bid these values. Not only should he pass two spades, but if the enemy persist to three hearts he should pass that too. Through his partner's daring action, the opponents have been pushed one trick higher—he must be satisfied with that. Otherwise, he will soon find his partners refusing to balance with him ever again.

Last, a word of warning about balancing: When you balance, you are relying to a great extent on the enemy bidding. Against opponents who habitually underbid, you are likely to find that cards which "must" be in partner's hand are in theirs. You may reopen and hear the enemy romp into a game that they had missed, or double you and inflict a painful penalty. True, this will result from *their* bad bidding not yours, but this is cold comfort. It is often better not to balance at all against players whose auctions you cannot trust. Remember, your opponents do not bid half so well as you. They have not, as you have, read this book right through to the end.